THE CHOICE

Living Your Passion Inside Out

Frank A. Thomas

HOPE FOR LIFE INTERNATIONAL BOOKS

17   16   15   14   13   1   2   3   4   5

ISBN-13 978-0-9820169-9-2

Printed in the USA

"When I heard that Frank Thomas was retiring as senior pastor after thirty-one years of church leadership, I was fascinated and intrigued. Frank is one of the most creative and leading thinkers in America today. I wanted to know his reason, rationale, and spiritual discernment that would allow this prominent pastor to retire in his prime. When I read this book, he took me through the process of living 'outside in' vs. 'inside out.' I clearly understood and said, 'This man is a spiritual genius.' I immediately followed the principles and began to put together my own plan."

—DR. GENEACE WILLIAMS, president
OLW Communications, Inc., Burr Ridge, IL

"Frank Anthony Thomas gives a cutting-edge model for answering the unasked question that plagues pastoral leadership, 'What's next?' Most clergy do not have a plan for life after pastoring, but I am developing one after reading this book. This is a must read for every clergyperson regardless of the stage of their career. Thomas is undoubtedly one of the leading thinkers for church and clergy in the country today. I believe this book will coach you to a roadmap for both ministry transition and passionate engagement in your life."

—DR. EUGENE L. GIBSON, JR., senior pastor
Olivet Fellowship/The Place of the Outpouring, Memphis, TN

"Frank Thomas is one of the most prominent thinkers and writers in this generation. In this book he takes the reader beyond the hype of church and ministry and gets down to the nuts and bolts of the challenges of ministry. He brilliantly shares his trials and triumphs within the decision-making process to follow his inner passion to leave the pastorate and join the academy. Within every sermon, Frank shares with us what he calls the backstory. I could not put this book down, as I am learning to live 'inside out.' This book merits our close attention."

—BISHOP CLAUDE R. ALEXANDER
The Park Church, Charlotte, NC

◆

"Frank Thomas' latest work, *The Choice: Living Your Passion Inside Out*, is nothing short of being a seminal work and a 'must read' for anyone interested in living his or her life to the maximum. So seldom do we as individuals, and for clergy, even less than that, stop and take the time to look inside ourselves and find out who we really are and what we were meant to do."

—DR. SUSAN SMITH
Columbus, OH

◆

"Last year for our revival, Frank Thomas preached three of the sermons in this book. My people and I were amazed at the depth, insight, and helpfulness of his message of 'inside out.' People are still quoting the messages. I recommend this book because Frank Thomas is one of the premiere preachers, pastors, scholars, and coaches of our time. Our people are waiting on this book because Frank mentioned it last year. I am so thrilled that it is finally out and many, many people can enjoy the deep spirituality in the concept of 'inside out.'"

—REV. DR. WILLIAM "BILL" LEE,
Loudon Avenue Christian Church, Roanoke, VA

◆

"With naked honesty, measureless humility, and seasoned scholarship, Thomas develops a confessional theology that can be compared with the disciplines of the late Howard Thurman, the saint with the calloused hands, who prayed daily Psalm 139 in its entirety. This book guides the head and heart of the reader into an activism of sacred passion in the lifelong journey of personal transformation, and is critically important for all persons who seek to possess and maintain the joy of living life more abundantly from the inside out. *The Choice* is a 'must' book to read and share with others."

—J. ALFRED SMITH, Pastor Emeritus
Allen Temple Baptist Church, Oakland, CA

◆

To my parents,

JOHN FRANK THOMAS AND
ALMETHA KING THOMAS,
who so marvelously facilitated
my splashdown
from the
eternal shore
and taught me:

If you do not ask,
the answer will always be no;

If you do not seek,
the treasure will never be found;

If you do not knock,
the door will never be opened;

If you do not go after what you want,
you will never have it.

Adapted from Matthew 7:7 and Patricia K. Suggs

CONTENTS

FOREWORD

The Choice, by preacher, pastor, professor, and widely published author Frank A. Thomas, is the best book that I have read on self-understanding and personal identity for a ministry of integrity that empowers the church for social transformation. With naked honesty, measureless humility, and seasoned scholarship, Thomas develops a confessional theology that can be compared with the disciplines of the late Howard Thurman, the saint with calloused hands, who prayed daily Psalm 139 in its entirety. This book guides the head and heart of the reader into an activism of sacred passion in the lifelong journey of personal transformation, and is critically important for all persons who seek to possess and maintain the joy of living life more abundantly from the inside out. The Choice is a "must" book to read and share with others.

Readers of the book will discover that the decision to leave the pastorate of Mississippi Boulevard Christian Church of Memphis, Tennessee, was not an impulsive leap into a blind future. Thomas shares very candidly the steps that he made with spiritual coaching to leave the pastorate of one of America's prestigious churches to live his passion inside out in honoring Jesus Christ. Careful reflection, conscientious prayer, and competent coaching from a credentialed life coach were enabling factors for defining and implementing the choice. Too often fatigue that saps passion, vision, and energy serves as the primary motivator for choosing to make a career change. Thomas suggests that persons called of God should make a clear distinction between a vocation and a job. A job is simply a legitimate way of earning money to pay bills for personal survival and the support of the family. However, a job often falls short of providing inner peace and joy that is found when we discover the joy of living from the inside out, the passion that God has planted into our hearts for ministry. Harlem Renaissance poet Countee Cullen talks about the nurture of the inner life, saying, "I live because an ember in me remembers to regain its fire, because what is and what has been not yet has conquered my desire. I live to prove the groping clod is surely more than simple dust; I live to see the breath of God beatify the carnal crust."[1]

In order for Thomas to make mature decisions that transcend popularity as pastor of a megachurch, he had to avoid being a divided self and make peace with himself. He surely prayed the prayer of Howard Thurman, "Give me the strength to be free and endure the burden of freedom and the loneliness of those without chains. Let me not be trapped by success, or by failure, nor pleasure, nor grief, nor malice, nor praise, nor remorse. Give me courage to go on. Facing all that waits on the trail . . ."[2] Making the correct choice is not easy.

Thomas also had to make sure that what we call our holy passions are not our egocentric wishes. Interests of personal welfare can tyrannize the lives of others with variables and vacillations of spiritual false ideals and spiritual fallacies. To define religion primarily as a quest for personal satisfaction is to miss the mission and meaning of Jesus' life. Thomas steers us away from petrifying the sacred with a subjectivity that is parochial, self-indulgent, and self-seeking.

If the foes of the Christian faith could, they would attack Thomas with the postmodern theory that defines religious faith as an attempt to "satisfy subconscious wishes so that belief in God is merely a projection of self-seeking emotions, an objectification of subjective needs."[3] But Thomas puts to rest such fallacious reasoning. His choice to live his passion inside out acknowledges Jesus Christ of the Gospels as the person who lived for others. So should our core Christian beliefs override subconscious egocentricity in order for us to live for others with the ultimate goal of unselfish preciousness.

The Choice is a clarion call to seek out a ministry life coach to provide direction and development. Such a person can assist in coping with ca-

---

1. Countee Cullen, *Color* (New York: Harper and Brothers, 1915), 106.

2. Howard Thurman, *A Strange Freedom* (Boston: Beacon Press, 1998), 34.

3. Abraham Joshua Heschel, *The Insecurity of Freedom* (Philadelphia: The Jewish Publication Society of America, 1966), 19.

reer choices, career building, career challenges, career changes, and in coaching ministry persons to finish well. Those who read about these concepts will be reminded that Moses was a spiritual life coach for Joshua, Deborah was a spiritual life coach for Barak, Mordecai was a spiritual life coach for Esther, Naomi was a spiritual life coach for Ruth, Paul was a spiritual life coach for Titus and Timothy, and Barnabus was a spiritual life coach for Paul and John Mark.

In 1944, Charles Scribner's Sons published the first edition of Reinhold Niebuhr's *The Children of Light and The Children of Darkness*, based on Luke 16:1–8. Niebuhr wrote that most proponents of democracy were children of light who had optimistic but naïve ideas about how society could be rid of evil. The children of darkness who were antidemocratic and ruthless had a sobering realism that the children of light needed. Adapting Niebuhr's argument for my own purpose in this preface, I maintain that if professional basketball coach Phil Jackson could coach Michael Jordan and Kobe Bryant into becoming superstars, what if clergy would not overburden the Holy Spirit as their counselor and allow an incarnation of spiritual life counseling to be actualized in a certified life counselor, as did the Reverend Doctor Frank Thomas?

If you want to deepen your personal walk with God, if you are desirous of taking an upward path leading to spiritual maturity, if you desire to be at peace with yourself and become more like Jesus of the Gospels, keep *The Choice* in your attaché case just as Martin Luther King Jr. did with *Jesus and the Disinherited* by Howard Thurman. If you want to learn as I am learning how to make the responsible choice, to define, execute, and release the choice, model the example of Thomas as your maneuvers for a meditative lifestyle that elicits from God Almighty the words, "You are the one in whom I am well pleased."

— J. Alfred Smith, Sr.

Pastor Emeritus, Allen Temple Baptist Church, Oakland, California; Distinguished Professor of Preaching and Church Ministries, American Baptist Seminary of the West and The Graduate Theological Union, Berkeley, California

STATEMENT OF CONFESSIONAL THEOLOGY

In his powerful foreword to *The Choice*, J. Alfred Smith, labels my work as "confessional theology." I had never viewed the material from this perspective, but his assessment struck me as insightful and true. I decided to look closer.

Generically, the term "confess" means to "give assent to," or "acknowledge." For Christians, the term echoes what Jesus said in Matthew 10:32 NIV, "Whoever acknowledges me before others, I will also acknowledge before my Father in heaven." Jesus mandated that we speak for him and the Christian principles that he lived and taught, especially in the face of persecution. Therefore, the church has had several strands of confessional theology across its history.

The first strand of confessional theology are the creeds and confessions of faith, whereby the church acknowledges and clarifies what it believes, often in the context of significant controversy and sometimes violence over dogma and interpretation.[4] Another aspect of confessional theology is when the church has made confessional statements that were not overtly political per se, but the implication of the confession was political in that it, for example, mandated that some form of mistreatment and abuse of human beings cease and desist.[5] This form of confessional theology believes that silence of the church in the face of evil is in fact complicity with evil. Many know this confession as the church in its prophetic role in the world. The third strand of confessional

---

4. Confessional documents that illustrate this point are the Nicene Creed (325), Augsburg Confession (1530), and Westminster Confession (1646).

5. Two confessional documents that illustrate the point are the Barmen Theological Declaration (1934) in Nazi Germany and the Belhar Confession (1986) during apartheid South Africa.

theology is the confession of sin after baptism to a priest that absolves or gives penance or reconciliation. Many are most familiar with this form of confession, where the intent is to restore right relationship with God and provide healing for the soul. The final strand of confessional theology is found in James 5:16, where James urges believers to confess their sin one to another. James believes that when we confess sin one to another and pray for each other in Christian community, we manifest healing in the lives of believers. James says, in this same verse 16, "the prayer of a righteous person is powerful and effective."

It is along the lines of this last aspect of confessional theology that I believe this book locates itself. When we confess one to another, we find healing for the soul. Specifically, I mean that we grow in Christ by acknowledging our positive and uplifting strengths, gifts, and accomplishments and by honest grappling, acceptance, and forgiveness of our faults, flaws, and mistakes. Fault, flaws, and mistakes are not things to be ashamed of or forever hidden; rather, they actually deepen us in the faith when given to God and "acknowledged" or "confessed." This form of confessional theology is anchored in Paul CONFESSING three times for his thorn in the flesh to be removed and God saying, "My strength is made perfect in weakness" (2 Cor. 12:7–11 NIV).

Based upon the fall of humanity, we are all morally flawed with the capacity to become whole, but until wholeness, we are works in progress. Many of us, as I am in this book, are working out unresolved family issues from our families of origin and/or cultural stigmas and prejudices that have labeled us and confined us. A friend told me about a gentleman who was raised without a father and spent his entire life searching for approval. He was a person who tried too hard to please others. "Once you understand this about him," my friend said, "he can more easily and comfortably be related to." Confessional theology is the place where we all can say that we are works in process: that we have salvation, but the work of sanctification is in process in our lives. As a matter of fact, the person who does not confess is living in a state of denial, hypocrisy, or pride, because the Christian faith at its heart is confessional.

As I was finishing the last chapters of *The Choice*, I began to read hip-hop artist and business mogul Jay-Z's critically acclaimed book *Decoded*.

According to the book jacket, "*Decoded* is a book like no other: A collection of lyrics and their meaning that together tell the story of a culture. An art form. A moment in history. And one of the most provocative and successful artists of our time."[6] In my reading of the book, it struck me as a form of confessional theology. As I thought more deeply about the book, I found I was able to come into more clarity about my book as confessional theology. I could not finish this "Statement of Confessional Theology" until I finished reading *Decoded*. The next paragraph is heavily influenced by the reading of the book.

Confessional theology is the interior space of a person's head, the discussion of the inner and complicated motivations that we face and confront on a daily basis and often do not speak, even to ourselves. We avoid confessional theology when we tell the story of success and rewards in ministry, such as megachurches, multiple degrees, voluminous speaking engagements, material accoutrements, etc., and do not talk about the sacrifices, pain, and the tremendous costs—first just to get to that point, and then even more to stay there. Jay-Z argues that when avoiding talking about the painful side, we are "telling a lie."[7] To preach the healing grace of God but never grapple honestly and publicly with despair in our own souls is to be disingenuous. To talk about blessings, miracles, and breakthroughs in the present and future tense, but only talk about our struggles in the past tense, according to confessional theology, is a form of evasion of the truth. Confessional theology does not force you to be a saint or a sinner, but it recognizes that you can be a believer and still have, as Jay-Z says, "unexpected dimensions and opposing ideals" or "your mind changes and wanders into strange, unexpected places."[8] Confessional theology acknowledges that we all have contradictions and moral complexity, because to have such is to be human. Confessional theology is not "insight," but "sight-in," the ability to see what is visible, to see inside the complexity in one's own soul.[9] In my estimation, confes-

---

6. Jay-Z, *Decoded*, (New York: Spiegel & Grau, 2011).

7. Ibid., 17.

8. Ibid., 240.

9. Ibid., 34.

sional theology is to be nakedly honest, or as they say in the hip-hop world, to "keep it real."

At its heart, confessional theology is an invitation to deep and meaningful relationship with others. In some sense, you do not really know me until you know my faults, flaws, and mistakes. Therefore, in my adaption of the insightful words of my colleague, Dan Moseley, I find the heart of what it means to be a growing Christian in this contemporary and often confusing world:

> I invite you into relationship with me as a wrestling, struggling, and limping human being and offer you space for your own confusions and struggles to resonate, not as shameful and embarrassing things, but as heroic or valid parts of the faith journey and story.[10]

I invite you into confessional theology.

---

10. Dan Moseley, *Healing Relationships: A Preaching Model* (St. Louis: Chalice Press, 2009), 40.

WORDS OF GRATITUDE AND THANKS

Special thanks to my family: my wife, Joyce, of thirty-six years; my son, Tony; and daughter, Rachel, for patience and encouragement every step of the way while Daddy was "researching and writing, again."

Special thanks to the Institute for Professional Excellence in Coaching (iPEC): Bruce P. Schneider, Luke Iorio, Elizabeth Fisch, Evie DiPiazza, Barb Heenan, and the entire iPEC family.

Special thanks to J. Alfred Smith, Sr. for his marvelous preface, unbridled support of this work, and naming it "confessional theology."

Special thanks for my mother and father, John and Almetha Thomas, and my sister, Angela Edwards, and brother, Frederick Thomas.

Special thanks to Vera Banks, Sallie Tipton, Kristin Firth, and Rick Porter, whose expertise and patience contributed mightily to making this book happen.

Special thanks to Jeremiah A. Wright, Jr., my pastor, who showed me vulnerability in the pulpit for the first time, which led to my understanding of confessional theology.

Special thanks to all my friends, colleagues, mentors, and mentees for the ways in which you have shaped my thinking and my life.

Special thanks to the families of the New Faith Baptist Church International of Matteson, Illinois, and the Mississippi Boulevard Christian Church of Memphis, Tennessee.

Special thanks to Darryl Simms and the team at MMGI Books for producing the first edition of this book. You were wonderful to work with.

Most of all, I thank God for the privilege of the ministry of the gospel of Jesus Christ.

INTRODUCTION

On July 2, 2012, I stood before the gathered congregation of the Mississippi Boulevard Christian Church of Memphis, Tennessee, at 6:00 PM and made this formal announcement: I hereby notify the church of my intent to retire as senior pastor as of December 31, 2012. Based upon their tremendous love, trust, and generosity in allowing me to be their pastor for thirteen years, I felt compelled to offer further explanation and therefore made these additional comments:

> I have suppressed the call to full time teaching for many years in order to serve as a pastor. In recent years, the call to academic life has become stronger and more present, and I began to seriously contemplate my retirement from pastoring to engage the teaching call on my life. After much prayer, it is clear to me that in the closing years of my ministry it is my life's work now to develop, mentor, encourage, inspire, and do whatever is necessary to cultivate a cadre of scribes and scholars, African American and otherwise, who are committed to transforming the world through sharing the genius of the African American preaching tradition.

I had dreaded making this announcement for months. However, I was surprised how clear and calm it came out, as if from somewhere deep inside. Despite my almost paralyzing anxiety at the conscious level, I was speaking from my inner core. Hours and hours of prayer, thought, reflection, Bible reading, devotion, discussion, discernment, consultation, coaching, and planning had brought me to this calm inner place where I knew what was true at my core. I named the experience as speaking "inside out."

Many members of the congregation were understandably shocked and grieved, though that night and beyond they were graciously and demonstrably supportive of my choice. The grieving and separation anxiety that started that night in both the congregation and myself was palpable in the room. Many people in the community, upon hearing the news, raised questions about how young and vibrant I appeared and expressed that they did not understand how "I could walk away in my prime." Several looked for nefarious motives. They believed that someone or some group was forcing me out. Several colleagues asked if I was under any pressure to resign by asking the question this way, "Are you all right?" They knew of far too many confrontations between clergy and congregations that often ended with the clergyperson resigning for another assignment, leaving quietly, or retiring as a sham or ruse to cover plays for power and control by laypersons, incessant criticism and hostilities by boards and committees, and negative and unresolved fighting and conflicts. One person asked me directly, "Were you forced to resign?" Of course, these people were looking "outside in" and had no idea that I was making an important attempt to live inside out. I was under no pressure from anyone from the outside. The pressure was from the inside to live and shape my life to respond to the deepest callings of my soul for the next period of my ministry.

In the sermons that follow, I lay out as much as I am able the transformative processes of inside out that led to my announcement that July night. Many of us are familiar with huge icebergs that reside in open water in the coldest climates. Because of the density of pure ice, scientists believe that typically only one-ninth of the volume of an iceberg is above water. The exact shape of the underwater portion can be difficult to judge by looking at the portion above the surface. This has led to the expression "tip of the iceberg," which denotes that what can be seen above the surface is indicative of much larger and deeper mass beneath the surface that cannot be seen. The sermons that follow are only the tip of the iceberg. The audible or written sermon is indicative of a greater mass that lies below the surface in the preacher and his/her intersection with life and the biblical text.

At the end of each sermon, in a section called "The Backstory," I describe the deep mass of my personal thoughts, struggles, and beliefs beneath the surface of the preached sermon. It is my hope that this approach will help the reader discover his/her backstory in response to the sermon. It is my hope that hearers listen and find that the sermons meaningfully speak to their backstories. It is only at the level of awareness of the backstory that deep change becomes possible in our lives. Indeed, it is only at the level of the awareness of the backstory that we can live inside out as opposed to living outside in.

Living inside out is a process that I will more fully flesh out in the succeeding pages. Let me offer a preliminary and summary explanation as I have discerned the process. First, we must come to acknowledge Jesus Christ at the inner core of our being. In this acceptance at our inner core, we come to know what we believe to be true. Only when we know what is true do we come to know what we want, really. Upon discovering what we want, really, our passion becomes clear to us. Once our passion is clear, it helps us to locate a deep need in the exterior world, and we discover the joy of a vocation, or what many of us know as a "call." Upon the discovery of this vocational call, we partner with God and discover work for our head, heart, hands, and feet to do. In doing this work, we discover that we must reengineer or re-create our entire lives, or we must do our creative best to reshape our entire lives to live out the vocational call.

This transformative process is what I call living inside out, and we all have the responsibility to create our lives from the inside out. Again, I will describe this concept more fully later. However, *The Message* version of Galatians 6:4–5 provides a perfect summary of the process:

> Make a careful exploration of who you are and the work that you have been given, and then sink yourself into that. Don't be impressed with yourself. Don't compare yourself with others. *Each of you must take responsibility for doing the creative best that you can with your own life.* (emphasis added)

Each of us has the responsibility to creatively shape and live our own lives from the inside out.

When I stood in front of the congregation of Mississippi Boulevard Christian Church and announced my retirement, I was living inside out. Beneath the conscious surface, deep forces of Spirit-guided passion and vocation were moving me to speak and change. The grief generated by the changes that the announcement forced was overwhelming. Alongside the grief was also the joy at finally being able to say what I had come to deeply believe. I believe my journey is indicative of the journey that we must all make. There comes a point in which we must make "the Choice." We must choose to live inside out or outside in.

Finally, in order to assist the reader, I have divided the book into four parts. In "Making the Choice" I explain that when one lives inside out, that is, when one accepts Jesus Christ at the core of one's being, one discovers the power of choice, which removes victim thinking, raises energy and engagement, and allows one to live according to "want to" rather than "have to." This part includes four sermons, "Get Up! Get Out! Get on with It!" "The Power of Choice: I Choose!" "From Victim to Victory!" and "Have to vs. Want To."

In the second part, "Defining the Choice," I explore the essential definition of inside out, which requires each person to answer two fundamental questions: 1) what do I know to be true at my inner core, and 2) what do I want, really. It is in answering these two questions that passion, energy, vocation, and ultimately authority flow from our inner core. This section includes "As One with Authority," "Amazing Grace," "A Basin, a Water Pitcher, and a Towel," and "Renew Your Yes!"

The third part, "Executing the Choice," explores inside out spirituality, that is, the redefining of one's spiritual life based upon living inside out. It gives practical suggestions for transition and leaving well. When we fully accept the power of choice, we redefine the concept of "lame duck" and find that it can be a wonderful time of healing, growth, and gratitude. Sermons in this section include "The Spiritual Ones," "The Spiritual Life," "Do You Have a Teachable Spirit?" and "No Hurt Like a Church Hurt."

The final part is "Releasing the Choice," and in many respects this is the most difficult section, dealing with the actual releasing of a call to be open to another call, which includes the painful saying of goodbye. Many of us do not do endings and leavings well, and this section faces our hesitance and fear head on. Sermons include "They Did Not Inquire of the Lord?," "If the Lord Is Pleased," "The Face of God," and "Leavings, Endings, and Letting Go."

My prayer is that this book and the scriptures, reflections, prayers, insights, and teachings contained herein will aid and assist you as you take responsibility "for doing the creative best that you can with your own life." We all have the power, creativity, opportunity, and responsibility to live inside out. I made "the Choice" and so can you.

part one

MAKING THE CHOICE

✦ I ✦

GET UP! GET OUT! GET ON WITH IT!

For this reason I bow my knees before the Father from whom every family in heaven and on earth takes its name. I pray that, according to the riches of his glory, he may grant that you may be strengthened in your inner being with power through his Spirit, and that Christ may dwell in your hearts through faith, as you are being rooted and grounded in love. I pray that you may have the power to comprehend, with all the saints, what is the breadth and length and height and depth, and to know the love of Christ that surpasses knowledge, so that you may be filled with all the fullness of God. —EPHESIANS 3:14–19 NRSV

After all this time, I haven't gotten over the agony of the life and death of Whitney Houston. The media reported that she struggled with addiction and with healthy life and living. There are many of us who also struggle with addictions and healthy life and living. Maybe not to the extent that Whitney did, and certainly not with the burden of the attention from paparazzi and the public's almost insatiable hunger for gossip and celebrity mishap, what I call "pop-culture trash." In other words, many of us struggle with healthy life and living, but we don't have paparazzi following us. We get to act out our sickness, illness, and moral failure without cameras, crowds, celebrity television and magazines, and public exposure. The bottom line is that many of us also struggle with healthy life and living just as Whitney Houston struggled.

I believe that at the heart of Whitney Houston's struggle is that she never really developed her inner core, the inner essence of her personhood. She never developed her inner being. She never came to fully know and understand her true inner life and the powerful resources inside her own soul. Many of us know how this feels because we have had experiences that interrupted the development of our inner core. For example, we saw too much violence and dysfunction too early, and what we saw interrupted the development of our inner core. We were inappropriately touched, taken advantage of, and even molested, and our sexuality was opened up to us before we were of age to make our own choices. While we were young and impressionable, we were ridiculed, bullied, heckled, rejected, despised, and called names like "stupid" or "dumb." We were either too fat or too skinny. We were too black or too light. Our hair was too kinky or it was too straight. Incessant insults were hurled at us about the way we looked or where we came from, and it interrupted our inner core development.

Or, for some of us, our parents abandoned us and did not raise us, and we struggle with a sense of abandonment. Some of us don't even know our father or mother, or maybe our father abandoned the home and our mother was left to struggle to survive, and poverty interrupted the development of our inner core.

Or our parents were addicted and wanted the addiction more than they wanted us, and it interrupted the development of our inner core.

Or the people in our house were dream killers, and whatever seed of hopes and dreams that we sought to live they snuffed out by negativity and criticism: *"You ain't going to be nothing, just like your daddy." "Your mama was a tramp and you're going to be a tramp, too."*

These are negative words and deeds tossed at us from people who were supposed to love us. This is nuclear warfare made upon a person's soul, and it interrupted the development of that person's inner core.

When the development of our inner core is interrupted, there is always something missing in the deep interior of our lives. And we look to fill what is missing on the inside by something that we find on the outside, what I call living outside in. Looking outside in for approval and affirmation, we ask, *"Am I good enough? Am I pretty enough? Will they like me?"* At the core, we are not as confident as we ought to be. We follow the crowd because we do not trust our own thoughts and feelings. We never really developed a true sense of our inner self and the ability to stand on our own. Seeking approval from the outside in, we reach outside of ourselves to fulfill the missing core. We live outside in rather than inside out.

And there are millions and millions and millions of people who live outside in. I believe that people who develop their core and live inside out are the exception to the rule. Most folk live outside in.

I was thinking about living inside out in my own life, and I heard Kevin Costner say this at the Whitney Houston home-going celebration:

> The Whitney I knew, despite her success and worldwide fame, still wondered; *Am I good enough? Am I pretty enough? Will they like me?* It was the burden that made her great and the part that caused her to stumble in the end (emphasis added).[11]

At hearing Costner's words, I immediately thought, Whitney, what do you mean, *are you pretty enough?* You are one of the most beautiful women in the whole world. You have millions of young girls who want to look like you and millions of men who want to be with you. And you're asking, *am I pretty enough?* You have a voice for the ages with millions of recordings sold and you are asking, *am I good enough?* You are a worldwide icon with fans on every continent following your every move and you're asking, *will they like me?* This is living life from the outside in; looking for approval from the outside for who we are on the inside. You cannot live a healthy life seeking what you do not already have on the inside. If you do not have it on the inside, you will not find it on the outside.

And, rather than condemn her, rather than feel sorry for her, after hearing Costner's words, I said, Me too, Whitney! Sometimes I struggle with the question: Am I good enough? Sometimes I struggle with: Am I handsome enough? Sometimes I struggle with: Will they like me? These questions and thoughts tempt me to live outside in. I ask you: How developed are you inside out? How developed are you at your inner core? Are you living inside out or outside in?

---

11. "Kevin Costner at Whitney Houston Funeral," http://www.youtube.com/watch?v=2wjh 0N1EzPI, accessed 07-22-12.

To help those of us who are living outside in, Paul wrote these words in our text for today, Ephesians 3:14–19. In AD 53, on the way home from his second missionary journey, Paul established the church at Ephesus. On his third missionary trip, Paul returned and stayed there for three years, preaching and teaching to build up the Ephesian church (Acts 19:1–20). A few years later, Paul was in prison under house arrest in Rome and was visited by various messengers, including Tychicus of Ephesus. Paul wrote a very encouraging letter to the Ephesian church and sent it by Tychicus. In the letter, Paul encourages those believers to understand the nature and purpose of the church as the living body of Christ in the world and how important it was to maintain the unity of the church. The book is full of love and the tenderness that Paul has in his heart for the Ephesian church. This love and tenderness is openly expressed when he says in Ephesians 3:14, *"For this reason I bow my knees before the Father."*

One of the most important acts of love is to pray for someone. How do we say that we love someone and yet not pray for them? How do you say you love me if you never go to the altar for me? Paul in this verse identifies the fact that he kneels and prays for the church. Bowing the knees, or kneeling, in this verse implies submissiveness to God. Kneeling implies an adoration and understanding of the power and the might of Almighty God. Paul loves the church and, out of his love for the Ephesian church, he prays for them.

For this reason I kneel before the Father from whom his whole family in heaven and earth derives its name (vs. 14–15 NIV). Paul acknowledges the glory and the majesty of the God to whom he prays. The one to whom he prays is the source of all creation, the rightful owner of everything and everyone in heaven and on earth.

For this reason I bow my knees before the Father, from whom every family in heaven and on earth takes its name. I pray that, according to the riches of his glory, he may grant that you may be strengthened in your inner being with power through his Spirit (vs.14–16 NRSV). Paul prays that, according to God's glorious riches, God would strengthen them with power through God's Spirit in their inner beings. The verb that Paul used in the Greek that's translated as "strengthened" is the opposite of the word "discouraged." God will encourage you at the depth and the core of your inner being! Paul says, "I fall on my knees before God—the one who made heaven and earth—and pray that God will strengthen you with God's glorious riches at the core, at the center, at the very essence of your life and inner being.

For this reason I bow my knees before the Father, from whom every family in heaven and on earth takes its name. I pray that, according to the riches of his glory, he may grant that you may be strengthened in your inner being with power through his Spirit and that Christ may dwell in your hearts through faith, as you are being rooted and grounded in love (vs. 14–17). God strengthens us in our inner being with power through the Holy Spirit, and what is the power of God's Spirit? The power, the glorious riches of the Holy Spirit, is the revelation of Jesus as the Christ. Paul prays that God, through the power of the Holy Spirit, may strengthen us in our inner being, and that we might be strengthened in the core and receive Christ in our hearts. Wherever the Holy Spirit is doing a strengthening work, the revelation of Christ accompanies the Holy Spirit, and Christ resides in the neighborhood of our hearts. Once Christ resides there, then you have the opportunity through faith to accept or reject the Christ that you find in your inner being. This is clear in verse 17: *So that Christ may dwell in your hearts through faith.* That by faith we may accept Christ and the glorious riches of God through faith!

And whenever you accept Christ by faith, guess what? Love shows up at your address. You see, the formula is that God sends the Holy Spirit to strengthen. And whenever the Holy Spirit strengthens, Jesus is revealed in the human heart! And whenever you accept Jesus through faith, love shows up! That's why the text says: *So that Christ may dwell in your hearts through faith, as you are being rooted and grounded in love.*

The result of the Spirit's penetration of your heart is that God will take up residence there. And when God takes up residence in your inner being, you will have faith in Jesus Christ. And when you have faith in Jesus Christ, you will come to know love. You will be rooted and established in love.

I pray that you may have power to comprehend, with all the saints, what is the breadth and length and height and depth, and to know the love of Christ that surpasses knowledge, so that you may be filled with all of the fullness of God (vs. 17–19). Now that we are rooted and grounded in love,

Paul prays that we might have the power to comprehend, which is to grasp, to hold on to as one's own, and to perceive the four dimensions of God's love. Paul is asking you to try to understand God's love, and then admits we can't understand it—God's love is incomprehensible. The four dimensions of God's love are incomprehensible and cannot be understood, and Paul tries to give us a few handles to understand it. Paul tells us that the love of God exemplified to the Gentiles is too large to be confined to any geometrical measurements, and then he tries anyway. He says God's love is wide and long and high and deep.

So how wide, Paul, is the love of God in Christ Jesus? I heard a preacher interpret what Paul said in this way: Paul says it's wide enough to reach the whole world and beyond. That's how wide the love of God in Christ Jesus is.

Well, Paul, how long is the love of God in Christ Jesus? He said it's long enough to stretch from eternity to eternity!

Well, Paul, how high is the love of God in Christ Jesus? Paul says it's high enough to raise Jews and Gentiles to heavenly places in Christ Jesus.

Well, Paul, how deep is the love of God? Paul says it's deep enough to raise people from sin's degradation and even from the grip of Satan himself.

Paul says this is how wide and how long and how high and how deep the love of God in Christ Jesus is, and to know this love surpasses all knowledge. Paul says: *For this reason I fall on my knees before the Father, the one from whom everything in heaven and earth derives its name. That God through the power of the Holy Spirit might strengthen you in your inner core*—in your inner being—*that you might accept Christ through faith and discover and be rooted and established in love and come to know how wide and how long and how high and how deep the love of God in Christ Jesus is; that you may live according to the measure of the fullness of Christ Jesus* (vs. 14–19). God's love surpasses—the text says—all knowledge, that you may live according to the full measure of all the fullness of Christ.

What is the measure of all of the fullness of Christ? You might be reading this and you have never really had the opportunity to develop your inner core. It might be that you are reading this asking, am I pretty enough? Am I smart enough? Will they like me? Am I good enough?

Maybe you are reading this and thoughts are flashing across your mind and your heart and you know that you, too, are just like Whitney Houston, struggling with life and healthy living. What I'm telling you is that the love of God in Christ Jesus comes down to the inner core. And if you are messed up in the inner core, you need to realize that the love of God in Christ is so high and so wide and so deep and so long that God would send God's Son to die for you. In that sacrificial act, you can realize how precious you are and how loved you are, and if God loves you, then you don't need approval from anybody else.

If somebody touched you before you were ready to be touched, and it interrupted the development of your inner core, the love of Christ comes down deep in your inner core and can heal that situation! Christ's love allows you to know how loved you are, how cared for you are. And you discover that your mama might not have given you what you really wanted and your daddy might not have acted like you really needed him to act, but that's all right! In Christ I've got everything I need! In Christ I'm all right! In Christ I'm encouraged! In Christ!

So I want to know why you're going around making excuses. Get up, get out, and get on with it!

When the text says living according to the fullness of the measure of Christ, it means that for whatever reason that your development was arrested in your inner core—whatever situation or circumstance never allowed you to develop a good sense of yourself and you're wondering: Am I good enough? Am I pretty enough? Will they like me?—in Christ, those inner wounds are healed. Get up, get out, and get on with it!

Kevin Costner closed his comments at Whitney Houston's home-going by saying, "Whitney, you're good enough." He set the scene that Whitney was now in heaven and God said, "Whitney, you're good enough." I appreciated him saying that. And everyone clapped at the home-going when he said it.

Oh, but I don't want to wait to get to heaven for God to tell me that I'm good enough. I want to be good enough on this side. I want to be pretty enough on this side. I want to be smart enough on this side. I want to be confident enough on this side. I want to be bold on this side. I want to walk in my authority on this side. I want to be blessed on this side. I want to overcome addictions on this side. I want to give up illicit behaviors on this side! I don't want to wait till I get to glory. That would be good, but it would be better on this side. Get up, get out, and get on with it!

So what are you waiting for? What is God telling you to do? What is God telling you to get rid of? What is God telling you leave? Where is God telling you to be bold? Where is God telling you to take a chance? Where is God asking you to step out on faith? Where is God asking you to move ahead, to go forward, to go to school or to get a business—to get up, get out, and get on with it?

You've been stalling long enough! You've got everything you need on the inside. Do I have to remind you? For this reason I fall on my knees before the Father, from whom everything on earth and in heaven derives its name. That God—according to God's glorious riches through the Holy Spirit—may strengthen you at your inner core. That you might find Christ there and accept Christ and, by your accepting Christ, love will live at your address. And you will know the love of God—how high and how wide and how deep and profound and long, and, most of all, you might learn to love yourself. That's called living inside out—not outside in—and living inside out is your privilege according the glorious riches in Christ Jesus. Get up, get out, and get on with it!

THE BACKSTORY

At the heart of this sermon is my struggle with the question of my authority. The question that the chief priests, teachers of the law, and elders asked Jesus is one of the central questions of my life: "By what authority are you doing these things, and who gave you this authority?" (Matt. 21:23 NIV, Mark 11:28, Luke 20:2). As a matter of fact, another sermon will directly focus on the discussion of Jesus and his authority as I continue to wrestle with the question of by what authority I have the confidence to act and direct my own life.

When a person—preacher or anyone—has not settled this authority question at the level of his/her inner being, the doubt gets formulated into the need for approval from the outside world and summed up in questions like: "Am I good enough? Am I pretty enough? Will they like me?" These questions pertain to all of us because they suggest that we need approval from someone or something to be secure and confident. Do we really need an outer voice? Whose outer voice?

And for how long do we need that voice before we come to accept our inner authority and heed our own inner voice?

While I professed that my authority was in God, at the deepest levels beneath the surface, human approvals were what I longed for and what I needed to function in my life. I began to consider the roots of this authority confusion and I remembered that for my eighth-grade graduation present my parents sent me and my cousin "down south" to Gulfport, Mississippi, to stay with my grandparents for a couple of weeks. When we got there, my uncle back in Chicago died of cancer, and we had to turn right around and go back to Chicago for the funeral. My grandparents rented a station wagon, one of those now old cars with the three seats in the back facing out the back window. My three cousins were in the back and they were cutting up and clowning; they were doing all kinds of crazy stuff kids do to have fun and pass the time. It was irritating my grandmother. She said, "Stop." They would quiet down for a minute and then continue with their irritating behavior. My grandmother then said, "Don't let me have to come back there." I was sitting in between my grandmother and my aunt in the middle seat facing the front of the car and had very little opportunity to participate in mischief. Finally, she got so irritated that she said, "Why don't you all be good like little Frank sitting here?" And all of a sudden, I felt special and I felt good, and I learned that to please people you have to be "good." It was a moment of arrested development: I learned that doing good and pleasing people is how you get approval, the authority to act in one's life. As best as I can tell, it was at that moment that I became acutely attuned to asking, Am I good enough? Am I pretty enough? Will they like me?

And being acutely attuned to those questions, I have spent a whole lot of my life being good. There is nothing wrong with that—being good has allowed me to accomplish much in my life and being good is the virtuous life that we should all lead to make a better world. But underneath being good was the question: by whose authority? Am I good because of Grandma and other authority figures in my life? Or am I good because I know good to be true and I adopt good as a value and the way I want to lead my life?

I am not able to detail it all yet, but in some sense the way I pastored was part of a need for approval. I began to wrestle with the question: what is my authority? When did I need approval by committees and the congregation? When, where, and how could I exercise my power and authority? What was my power and authority? I was even so unsure that I began to question by whose authority I became a pastor in the first place. I will say much more about this later, but I was not at ease in my sense of authority in my personal life or in my pastoral life. I was living life outside in rather than inside out. My life began to feel like a weight and a heavy burden.

However, when I read the Ephesians 3:14–19 text, I felt hope. Though Paul was talking to the Ephesian church, I took the text personally—that Paul was praying for me to be strengthened in my inner being through the power of the Holy Spirit; that Christ would dwell in my heart through my faith in Jesus; that I, being rooted and grounded in love, would come to know how long and high and wide was the love of God in Christ Jesus; that knowing that love, I could be filled to the measure of all of the fullness of God. It meant for me that through Christ I could come to love myself and, in the confidence of that love, be my own authority. I would no longer ask, "Am I good enough?" "Am I pretty enough?" "Will they like me?" Those questions have been settled in the love of Christ Jesus that I received at my inner core. I am asking the Holy Spirit to strengthen me at my inner core to live inside out. I continue to tell myself: get up, get out, and get on with it! I tell myself that I have everything I need on the inside. I can live inside out.

2

THE POWER OF CHOICE: I CHOOSE!

We do not lose heart. Though hourly we are wasting away, yet
inwardly we are being renewed day by day. For our light and
momentary troubles are achieving for us an eternal glory that
far outweighs them all. —2 CORINTHIANS 4:16–17 NIV

Several weeks ago, I was invited to deliver a lecture at a symposium and celebration of the ministry and preaching of Fred B. Craddock, a contemporary American preaching genius. Craddock turned the Euro-American preaching world on its head with a revolutionary, inductive preaching method that led him to be selected as one of the twelve best preachers in the English-speaking world.

As I was preparing for the lecture, I recalled that when I was pastoring in Chicago, I invited Dr. Fred Craddock to be our revival preacher. We called the event "The Festival of Preaching," to which we invited the very best preachers from around the country, and Dr. Fred Craddock certainly fit that criterion. I sent the letter of invitation and Dr. Craddock graciously consented to come. I put Dr. Craddock's picture in marketing materials to the congregation and the community. The response was swift and sure: "Pastor, I am sure that Dr. Craddock is a fine preacher, but everyone knows that black preachers are the best preachers and make the best revivalists." People went on to say, "We want a stir-us-up, stomp-down black preacher to fire us up and revive our hearts." I persisted and held my position because I know good preaching when I hear it, and Fred Craddock was a powerful preacher. Swimming against the tide of public opinion, I ended up begging and pleading with the congregation to come out the first night to the revival. Based on their stereotypes of what was good preaching, I was worried that they would not come.

Well, as a result of my pastoral pleading, we were able to get the house full for that first night. Dr. Craddock came out, and the first situation was that the pulpit was too tall. I was embarrassed that I had missed this detail of planning until Dr. Craddock said, "Frank, I think your pulpit is made for adults." And he laughed, and we laughed, and it was on from there. The congregation came back the next night and the next night, and when Dr. Craddock finished, the response was that same response that was said of Jesus in Mark 12:34, "No one dared ask him any questions."

Well, Fred Craddock preached his last official sermon October, 2011. He is eighty-three years old and afflicted with Parkinson's disease. This preaching giant, one of the top twelve preachers in the entire English-speaking world, was being silenced by Parkinson's. I have been grieving the preaching of Fred Craddock. Not that he is dead, but grieving the loss of his preaching voice and his insight into the biblical text and life.

This 2 Corinthians 4:16–17 text comes to mind when I think about Fred Craddock: Outwardly we are wasting away. This is not a sermon to generate sympathy for Fred Craddock. He is doing fine and would have it no other way. This is a sermon for all of us because sooner or later it will also happen to all of us. We will all waste away. I'm not suggesting that all of us will get Parkinson's, but we will get something. Some of us will get cancer. Some of us will be afflicted with dementia. Some of us will have a heart attack. For some of us it will be a stroke. For some of us it will be diabetes. And if not this level of serious illness, we will at least discover that we cannot do what we were once able to do and move like we were once able to move. I have compassion for people being pushed in wheelchairs because that will probably be me one day. Much of this comes with old age, and if we live long enough, old age will come to us all. As the old folks used to say to us as kids when we were making fun of their old age—"Just keep on living. Keep waking up and keep going to bed." Like it or not—we are all wasting away.

Maybe you're watching someone you love struggle with wasting away, so you know what I mean when I say I'm grieving the voice of Fred Craddock. Or maybe in the past you have had to watch someone you love diminish. Do you remember somebody who was a giant to you and then you had to change his/her diaper? Do you remember somebody who was the strongest of the very strong to you and you looked up and life transition happened and now he/she is the child and you are the parent? It happens to all of us. I hate to think about it, but maybe someday someone will change my diaper. I guess that is one of the reasons I should be kind to my wife and daughter (smile). Outwardly, we are wasting away every day.

When Paul looks at his outer self, he realizes that he's wasting away. He is remembering all of the hardships on his outer self because of his proclamation of the gospel. His body has been damaged by all the suffering he has endured for the sake of the gospel. Paul says in 2 Corinthians 11:23–28 (NIV):

> I have worked much harder, been in prison more frequently, been flogged more severely, and been exposed to death again and again. Five times I received from the Jews the forty lashes minus one. Three times I was beaten with rods, once I was stoned, three times I was shipwrecked, I spent a night and a day in the open sea, I have been constantly on the move. I have been in danger from rivers, in danger from bandits, in danger from my own countrymen, in danger from Gentiles; in danger in the city, in danger in the country, in danger at sea; and in danger from false brothers. I have labored and toiled and have often gone without sleep; I have known hunger and thirst and have often gone without food; I have been cold and naked. Besides everything else, I face daily the pressure of my concern for all the churches.

Paul had suffered for the gospel and it had taken a toll on his outer self. He could have been angry, bitter, vengeful, and retaliatory about the cost of spreading the gospel. He could have engaged in self-pity, a reluctance to pray, a spirit of boasting and self-righteousness, and a strident cowardice to speak for Jesus. He could have been a victim. Paul realized that, just like all of us, outwardly he was wasting away, and even more so because of the gospel.

And this would be very bad news indeed, except the Apostle Paul contextualizes the situation and says: *Therefore, we do not lose heart.*

Though outwardly we are wasting way, yet inwardly we're being renewed day by day. What Paul means is that our only hope in life is to be renewed day by day. Our only hope in life is to be renewed inwardly day by day—what I call living inside out. The only hope we have is that the Holy Spirit will renew our spirits, build our spirits, strengthen our spirits day by day at our inner core that we would live inside out.

Traditionally, Christians make a critical distinction between flesh and spirit. I believe this text modifies this traditional understanding in that Paul conceives of the Christian as having two distinct selves. There is a reality that he refers to as the outer self, or what I call living outside in. He means that his body, mind, and emotions are experiencing the temptations and the contaminations and the sinful morality of this present world. This represents victim thinking or living outside in when we ask outside-in questions: Am I pretty enough? Am I smart enough? Will they like me? The outer self is always looking for approval according to the standards and dictates of the outside world.

Paul is also speaking of the inner self, and by that he means all that we have become through being joined to Jesus Christ through accepting Christ as our savior. He is referring to his new status in Christ that we discussed in the last sermon, where the Ephesians 3 text said God strengthens us in Christ Jesus in our inner being according to the divine resources and energy of the Holy Spirit. By virtue of being reborn as a child of God, there is a spiritual power working on the inside that Paul suggests is renewing him day by day. This power makes Paul a partaker of the divine nature, and because of this divine nature, he can choose to live inside out rather than outside in. We can choose to focus on decay and wasting away on the outside or being renewed from inside every day by the power of the Holy Spirit.

The divine nature on the inside and at the core of our inner self gives us the power to choose. When you are a victim, you do not have the power to choose. Somebody has already chosen for you. As a victim, you give other people power to choose and decide for you. As a reborn child of God, you have the power to choose. Paul is suggesting that Christ's inner nature gives the Christian the power to choose the life he/she wants—to be renewed every day by the power of choice and to live inside out.

These two natures characterize every Christian—what we are outwardly, or outside in, and what we are inwardly, inside out. All of us as followers of Christ Jesus wrestle with these dynamics throughout our lives, and we have the choice—the inner versus the outer, inside out versus outside in. Are you going to live inside out or are you going to live outside in? Are you going to take the responsibility and authority that God has given you by virtue of being reborn in your inner life and live according to the measure of the fullness of Christ? Or are you going to back down in a corner and play victim and talk about what you don't have and what you can't do, and what you can't accomplish, and what you can't achieve, and who's blocking you and who's stopping you and who's making you mad? Are you going to seek the approval of people for what you want to do or be in your life, or are you going to get in Christ and make a choice as to what you want to be in your life?

When you move from being a victim and live inside out, you're making daily progress in the new life that God has given you. When you live life inside out, your trust in God is stronger. Our convictions about the gospel are deeper. Our wisdom in knowing ourselves and our ability to overcome the troubles of the world are more profound. Our resistance to sin is more determined. Paul appeared to be a fading old, sick man, but inwardly he was effectually transformed day by day. His inner youth was being renewed like the eagle.

What Paul is saying is that the gospel gives you the power to choose. You can choose the inner life. With Christ in your life you can choose the life you want to lead. I want to offer several principles based upon my reflections on this text and living life from the inside out to help you live inside out. The first principle of inside out is to develop your character first, and then your gifts. God wants to develop your character first, and then raise your gifts to the level of your character. However, what we tend to want to do is develop our gifts first and then work on our character later. God wants inside out, and we want outside in.

Some of us are more concerned about our gifts and the exposure of our gifts than we are about our character. But if you're not careful, your gifts will take you beyond your character, and when your gifts take you beyond your character, you end up in moral fault and trouble. As a result,

God will not put you on some stages until you develop your character. God works inside out; we want to work outside in. We want to get a public re-altions specialist, a marketing plan, a publicist, and an image consultant to increase our exposure. We want to make it big! We want to make a name for ourselves! We want the allure of fame and fortune and what goes with it—cash, cameras, and crowds. Fame and fortune without character will lead to moral failure. Fame and success without character will lead to addictions and behaviors that embarrass our faith. God starts with character first and then your gifts, because character is on the inside and gifts are your expression of your character on the outside. We must live inside out.

The second principle of the inside out life is this: the gospel frees you from what people think of you, but, more importantly, it frees you by freeing you of what you think of yourself. When you get free from what you think of yourself, it doesn't matter what other people think about you.

The key issue in life is what you think of yourself, and you attract to yourself what you think of yourself. What you think of yourself is who you are on the inside. What you think of yourself will cause you to attract people who think the very same thing of you. So if you don't think much of yourself, you attract people who don't think much of you. If you think low of yourself, you attract people who think low of you. If you're leading a miserable life, you attracted it. If you have a miserable job, you attracted the job to yourself. If you have miserable friends, that's who you attracted. If you have a miserable spouse, that's who you attracted. We need the gospel to free us from what we think of ourselves!

That's why it's important that you understand how high and wide and long and deep the love of God in Christ Jesus is, so that you may live according to the full measure of Christ. The love of Christ has to come down to my very core and free me of what I think about me!

Finally, the third principle of the inner life is that every situation is an opportunity. Regardless of what happens to us in life, we can take it, mold it, and shape it into an opportunity. When you have the power of choice, you look at every situation as an opportunity. What's the opportunity here? Rather than complaining, whining, being depressed and down—what's the opportunity here? And when you look for the opportunity, you are living life inside out.

In a very difficult time in my ministry as a pastor, in my pain and frustration, I wrote this: *Pastoral work has been and always will be hard and is a heavy weight and burden around my neck.* That was the statement of a victim, which expressed what I thought about myself. I was living outside in. I did not think that I had a choice. I did not believe that I could change this reality of the burden and weight of ministry, and I was trapped.

To live inside out, I had to reframe that statement by saying, "I choose." I have discovered that whenever I say "I choose," my own inner power and authority come into the situation and I find opportunity. "I choose" exercises the power of choice and creates opportunity in any situation. I had to reframe the statement as an "I choose" statement: *In response to God's call, I choose to be a pastor because it allows me to inspire, encourage, touch, and teach many and enables me to express my values of growth, service to God, and commitment to my family.*

Now, how did that second statement feel in comparison to the first one? The first one expresses that pastoral work is hard, a weight, and woe is me. I'm beaten down. I'm trapped. No! I choose to be a pastor. I exercise the power of choice. I chose to be a pastor and there is opportunity before me. Pastoral work has allowed me to inspire, encourage, touch, and teach many as well as enabled me to express my values of growth, service to God, and commitment to my family. I choose to be a pastor! That's from the inside out with the power of choice. I choose!

You have the ability to reframe your reality by the power of choice. Jesus Christ from the inside out gives you the power to choose a different reality. You don't have to settle for being a victim. You don't have to settle for whining and complaining and being broke and bankrupt, being disrupted, being stopped, being blocked, being down, being depressed, and being a slave to the past. You don't have to do that. You have a choice. You can create the world in which you live by the power of choice.

And, when you allow God to come down to your inner core and change the way that you view you, you will attract to yourself powerful opportunities. When you and I allow Christ to come down in the depths and core of our being, and we allow Christ to change how we view ourselves, such that we realize the authority and the power that we have to live according to the full measure of Christ, then powerful opportunities will come our way. When you make that choice, you attract to yourself powerful opportunities. You don't have to find opportunity; opportunity finds you! Meditate deeply on this question: When was the last time a powerful opportunity found you? Outwardly we are wasting away, but the power of choice renews us inwardly day by day.

THE BACKSTORY

Preachers are often guilty of presenting scriptural solutions but not adequately detailing the true inner work that it takes for the hearers to arrive at the resolutions that we suggest. Preachers are sometimes like the math teacher who puts the answer to the problem on the board and never slows down to show the step-by-step process to arrive at the solution. In this version of the backstory, I would like to give you the sense of the real inner work that it took to live the power of choice in my life.

As the following diagram illustrates, life is filled with neutral activating events (NAE).[12] Life will presents us with events, happenings, circumstances, and situations that are in reality completely neutral. These events are called activating because they require a response from us, and when we supply a response, we give meaning or interpretation to them. How we interpret, or supply meaning, to NAE is based upon our core thought. Our core thought could be victim, conflict, responsibility, reconciliation, peace, love, joy, etc. Once our consciousness assigns a core thought, then a core feeling is produced. The core feeling is directly related to core thought. For example, the core thought of the victim mentality might produce the core feeling of apathy. The core feeling then produces an action/result. For example, the core feeling of apathy might produce the action/result of lethargy and hopeless inactivity. The generic process looks like this:

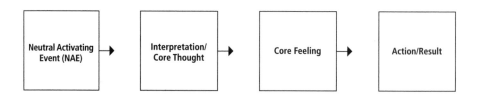

---

12. While the term "neutral activating event" is mine, the concept of core thought, core feeling, and core action is known as the Energetic Self-Perception Chart (I Chart) and belongs to Bruce D. Schneider, *Energy Leadership: Transforming Your Workplace and Your Life from the Core* (Hoboken, NJ: John Wiley & Sons, 2008), 15.

It is at the point of interpretation that our core thought gives an event, and subsequently our lives, meaning. It is at the point of core thinking that we choose the life that we want to live. For example, earlier I stated that I wrote this statement: "Pastoral work has been and always will be hard and is a heavy weight and burden around my neck." If we diagram it out, then my statement looks like this:

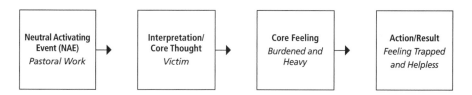

Based upon my core thought of being a victim, my response to pastoral work was feeling burdened and weighted down, resulting in the conviction that I was trapped and helpless. The only way to change my perspective was to change my core thought. When I changed my core thought to "I choose," the statement became: "In response to God's call, I choose to be a pastor because it allows me to inspire, encourage, touch, and teach many as well as enables me to express my values of growth, service to God, and commitment to my family." The diagram of the "I choose" statement looks like this:

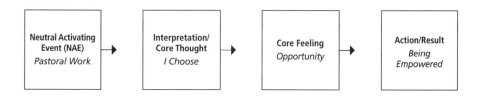

It is when I changed my core thought that I changed my core feeling, and my action changed as a result. My point is that we control our interpretation and the meaning that we assign to any event in life. We control how we think about a situation. How we think core thoughts is about our consciousness, the sum total of our thoughts, beliefs, and emotions, in the present moment and the past. When I suggest that God encourages us according to God's glorious riches in Christ Jesus, I mean that faith in Jesus Christ would reside, and therefore change and adjust, our core thought, the sum total of our thoughts, beliefs, and emotions, in the present moment and the past.

Let me give an example of first a statement, then a reframed statement applying faith in Christ to help change the direction of a life.

STATEMENT:

Because I failed the exam, I cannot do anything.
I am totally worthless and incompetent and cannot even possibly motivate myself to take the exam again.

REFRAME:

I choose to believe Phil. 4:13: "I can do all things through Christ who strengthens me."

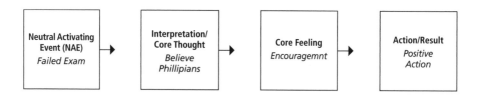

Based upon our core thinking, we give meaning to a failed exam. In my relationship with Jesus Christ, I have the authority to make every NAE into a positive opportunity in my life. This is the power and authority I have when Christ resides in the core of my inner being.

3

FROM VICTIM TO VICTOR!

You have heard that it was said an eye for an eye and a tooth for a tooth. But I tell you do not resist an evil person. If anyone slaps you on the right cheek, turn to her the other cheek also. And if anyone wants to sue you and take your outer shirt, give him your T-shirt as well. If anybody forces you to go one mile, go with that person two miles. Give to the one who asks you and do not turn away from the one who wants to borrow from you.

—MATTHEW 5:38–42, PARAPHRASED

I have been doing a tremendous amount of thinking about being a victim. In fact, my spiritual goal for the year is to erase absolutely every ounce of victim thinking from my life. I have discovered that victim thinking injects negative energy into my body, mind, and soul. I have discovered that when I operate in any area of my life using victim thinking, I come to believe that I'm powerless . . . hopeless . . . helpless . . . desolate . . . lonely . . . abandoned . . . and insecure, with sorrow, depression, grief, and guilt operating throughout my life. When I operate out of a victim perspective, I believe that this one has done this to me and that one has done that to me. This one doesn't like me. That one has it out for me. In other words, I give my power and authority over to somebody outside of myself to shape my destiny and my world.

Victim thinking is dangerous because it forces us to blame other people for our unhappiness. We think thoughts like these: If my spouse were a better spouse, I would be a better marriage partner; if my pastor were a better pastor, I would be a better Christian; if my parents had been better parents, then I'd be a better person right now. When I think like this, I don't take any responsibility for the quality and the tenor of my life. I don't take any responsibility for the fact that happiness is an inside job and nobody controls my inner world but me. I ignore the fact that I feel like I feel because I choose to feel that way. I feel like I feel because I decide to feel that way. I don't take responsibility for my emotions or my life. I'm a victim—a victim of my own emotions!

Let me quickly define the word "victim." To be a victim is to be subject to something or someone in a negative way. When I say "victim," you probably think that I'm talking about somebody who is/was in an abusive relationship. It is a very sad fact in our world that many children are victims of abuse and correspondingly there is far too much abuse of women. But, when we define the word in those narrow terms, it lets many of us off the hook, because we might not have ever been in an abusive relationship or abused as a child. A broader definition is to be subject to thoughts, beliefs, emotions, and perceptions that work against you, don't serve you well, or stop you from doing something that God would have you to do. Many of us are victims to thoughts and feelings and emotions that are hindering us and holding us back.

I will say this again and again because this is such an important principle for living inside out: many of the events in life are neutral, neither good nor bad, until you give them an interpretation. Your consciousness is what gives events in life interpretation. And when you have "victim" as part of your consciousness and your thinking, you supply a victim interpretation to the neutral events of life. You interpret life such that you are subject to and controlled by the events of life. An alcoholic is subject to alcohol and the alcoholic's life is controlled by alcohol. The drug addict is subject to drugs and his/her life is controlled by drugs. To be subject to something is to be controlled by it.

Some of us are victims of past relationships. That is, what has happened in a past relationship is controlling what's happening now. Some of us are victims of past feelings and past emotions that are controlling us in the present moment. Somebody is a victim of an unhappy home, a victim of a painful marriage, a victim of prejudice and terrible injustice. There are victims of messed-up finances. There are victims of anger, victims of violence, and victims of fear. And, Lord knows, there are victims of painful experiences in the church! Somebody won't serve today because he/she had a painful experience in church.

There are people who are victims of illness, sickness, and disease. It's possible to have cancer, but it is a different thing to be a victim of cancer. Or, as a friend of mine said to me as she was awaiting the results of a biopsy and the possibility of recurring cancer, "I'm going to live until I die. What I won't do is die while I'm still living." There are victims of senseless violence. There are victims of hatred and prejudice. Ultimately, you are not a victim of the events of life, but a victim of how you think and feel about the events and things that happen in life. Some people allow themselves to be subject to life, and other people decide and determine their perspective and how they are going to respond to the neutral activating events in life.

There are so many victims and so many who are subject to life. We're not choosing our emotions; we're not controlling our destiny; we're not dictating the direction of our life. We're subject to life. We are living life outside in. Could you be honest today and admit to God that you're playing the role of victim in some aspect of your life? Can you be honest and tell God that you have given over your power and inner authority to a force that's not Jesus Christ? Can you admit you've been blaming, that you've been making excuses? Can you be honest today about living subject to life?

You can be honest today because Jesus loves victims. Jesus takes victims and turns them into victors. Jesus loves victims and it is right here in today's text in Matthew 5:38–42. Let's explore what the text means.

Matthew 5:38–42 is set in the discourse of the Sermon on the Mount. Jesus, of course, is a master teacher and is laying down truth for a life that is pleasing to God. The unifying theme of the Sermon on the Mount is the kingdom of heaven. In Matthew 4:17–23 (NIV), Matthew introduces the primary content of Jesus' teaching and preaching as the gospel of the kingdom of heaven:

From that time on Jesus began to preach, "Repent, for the kingdom of heaven has come near." . . . Jesus went throughout Galilee, teaching in their synagogues, proclaiming the good news of the kingdom, and healing every disease and sickness among the people.

After Matthew explains that the essence of the message of Jesus is the kingdom of heaven breaking into earth, next is an explanation of the ethics of the kingdom. The Sermon on the Mount includes ethical guidelines for people who belong to the kingdom of God. It is a glimpse of how our lives should be filled with love and grace if we belong to the kingdom of God.

Jesus says in Matthew 5:38: *The law says it's an eye for an eye and a tooth for a tooth.* In the language of the world, we call this tit for tat. You get mad at me or hurt me and I'm going to hurt you. You cuss me, and I'm going to cuss you. You take out one of mine, and I'm going to get one of yours. It's gangster and gang warfare in life. You bother me, and I'm going to bother you. It may take me a long time; it may take me awhile; it may take me a minute—but if you did that, I'm going to get you. We are all familiar with tit for tat or an eye for an eye and a tooth for a tooth. Tit for tat has a lot of emotional vengeance and harmful behavior to community in it.

Jesus means that if someone does something wrong to you, don't strike back, but let the judiciary administer the return slap. Jesus is arguing out of Exodus 21:24, Leviticus 24:19–20, and Deuteronomy 19:21. The idea of an eye for an eye was for the justice system to administer justice and not for the injured person to administer justice. If you read the context, it was to take vengeance out of the equation of human relationships and put the mandate for punishment on the nation's judicial system. The goal was to terminate personal vendettas because they're so emotional, so violent, and so destructive of community. Jesus says the kingdom lifestyle is that, if somebody strikes you, you don't just strike back! You allow the justice system and/or God to finish the business, because personal vendettas and subjective vengeance will break community and short-circuit your blessings from God.

So this text is not about not to hit somebody back! This text is about removing vengeance from human relationships. Jesus' meaning is this: Do not resist an evil person with vengeance. He's not saying don't resist evil. If civil rights workers had not resisted evil during the civil rights movement, social progress would not have been made. Jesus is not just saying give a free pass to evil; he means don't let vengeance be the motive of your resistance, because God ultimately is the one who sees and hears. The Bible says in Romans 12:19, "Do not take revenge, my dear friends, but leave room for God's wrath, for it is written: 'It is mine to avenge; I will repay,' says the Lord."

In verse 39, Jesus gives the first of four illustrations to clarify his initial point in verse 38: *If anyone slaps you on the right cheek, turn to them the other cheek also.* This is a painful and insulting blow. The assumption in the text is that a right handed person strikes somebody on the right cheek. In the neighborhood I grew up in, it was called a backhand slap. Now it was one thing when somebody slapped you with an open palm; but when somebody backslapped you it was the height of an insult, and to save face and preserve one's dignity, one was duty bound to attack and fight to the last. The backhand slap was the ultimate insult. Jesus says do not attack; give them the other cheek also.

In verse 40, Jesus says: If anyone wants to sue you and take your outer shirt, give him your cloak as well. If somebody sues you for your inner garment, give them your T-shirt as well. According to Mosaic law, the outer cloak was an inalienable possession (Exod. 22:26; Deut. 24:13). But Jesus is saying that if one of the followers of Jesus was sued for his tunic (an inner garment like our suit, but worn next to the skin), far from fighting in court, he should gladly part with what he may legally have the right to keep. Jesus reinforces the same principle as verse 39.

Jesus says in verse 41: If anybody forces you to go one mile, go with them two miles. This verse is indicative of the Roman practice of commandeering civilians to carry the luggage of military personnel a prescribed distance. Any military personnel or Roman soldiers could make civilians carry their luggage a Roman mile. Jesus is saying that if a Roman soldier makes you carry the luggage one mile, carry it another mile. Again, the same principle is being taught as in verse 38 and 39.

Jesus says in verse 42: *Give to the one who asks you and do not turn away from the one who wants to borrow from you.* The meaning here is that Jesus requires interest free loans (Exod. 22:25, Lev. 25:37) and a generous spirit (Deut. 15:7-11). In this final illustration Jesus makes plain the meaning of the entire pericope—generosity. Let me give an example to make Jesus' meaning clear in our contemporary time. You have a family member, a cousin, who has bad credit, who wants to buy a luxury automobile, and he calls and asks for a substantial loan. Despite his bad credit and inability to pay it back, Jesus says give it to him interest free and without anger and resentment, but generously! The point of this illustration and all four illustrations is generosity.

Now there's a great debate as to whether Jesus means for us to take these four illustrations literally, such as, he means for us to give to everyone who asks. We cannot take this to the extreme such that we are a soft touch for anybody who has a need. Or Jesus is saying to the person who's being abused in a relationship that if you get backslapped in an abusive relationship, turn the other cheek and take another slap. I believe that if you're being abused in a relationship, you get the hell out of there to save your life. No one deserves to be abused. This is not what Jesus means.

What's happening in this text is that Jesus is providing us a mandate to not be a victim. There is something about generosity that takes us out of being a victim. When I choose to be generous in the face of the possibility of being a victim, I move from the realm of victim to victor. The choice for generosity removes personal vendetta and the need for vengeance from human relationships and I can choose how to respond, even allowing the justice system to render the slap. Generosity and love is at the heart of nonviolence. Jesus is not advocating nonresistance, he is advocating the removal of vengeance and the possibility of creative generosity and love, which can be defined as nonviolence. Generosity takes me out of the victim position and brings victory into my life.

Jesus has to use such vivid illustrations to almost shock us into the reality of generosity's ability to make us victorious. He has to do so because it's attractive to be a victim. When you're a victim you don't have to take responsibility. It's hard work to take responsibility. It's hard work to admit to yourself that you let yourself down. It's hard work to admit I was wrong. It's hard work to say I messed up. It's hard work to take responsibility without excuses. We don't like that feeling when we admit to ourselves that we've dropped the ball.

A victim is somebody who excuses himself/herself from being held accountable. Victims never have to make decisions. They don't make decisions; they let decisions make them. They stall, or there are so many options that they can't decide. So they don't make a decision. They let the deadline pass, and once the deadline passes, the decision has already been made. They don't make decisions. You see, when I make decisions, I have to live with the consequences of my decisions. When I make a decision, I have to choose. And when I have to decide something, I have to cut some option out. When you cut something out, you have to live without that which you cut.

When you're a victim, you don't have to make decisions as those with power and responsibility do. People who have power and responsibility have tough decisions to make. Do you realize that when George Herbert Bush signed the order that bombs would be released in the Gulf War, he said he lost sleep that first night and many nights thereafter, because he knew that, by virtue of a pen stroke, he was sending young men and women to a battle place that would result in some loss of life. That's great responsibility.

I am not sure that we want that kind of responsibility. I am not sure that we want that kind of authority. We really don't want that kind of authority over our own lives—let alone over a whole lot of people's lives. Victim—we like it. We like it. I can be excused. There's something attractive about being a victim. I can be excused from the responsibility of making choices about my life.

Victim thinking is a sickness because being a victim allows me to celebrate my failings. In other words, I celebrate my losing. I justify my weaknesses and shortcomings by saying that I'm a sincere person. I celebrate my failings and use my incapacity to say that I'm really a good person. I live beneath my dignity and worth because I rationalize and justify to myself that I'm a good person. Jesus is encouraging us to refuse to be a victim. He's saying that being a victim leads to a need for vengeance to feel better. If somebody slaps me on my cheek, I'm not a victim! Here's the other cheek! If you sue me for my shirt, I'm not a victim! Here's my cloak. If you make me go one mile, I am not a victim! I choose to go another mile! Generosity takes you out of being in a victim position. It's my choice how many miles I walk.

It would appear that Jesus was a victim. If there ever was a victim, the cross at Calvary makes Jesus look like a victim. I heard an old preacher tell this story: There was a meeting in heaven, a divine business meeting between God the Creator, Jesus, and the Holy Spirit. Weren't but three people in existence at the time and they decided to have a meeting. The Creator God called the meeting to order and asked the Holy Spirit to read the minutes from the last meeting. The minutes from the last meeting were read, seconded, and adopted. There seemed to be an agenda item in the old business that was tabled to be discussed at the next meeting. This agenda item was God the Creator's decision to bring a motion to the floor to create human beings. In the discussion about the matter, God the Creator proposed that human beings would have free will. The Holy Spirit raised the question that if they had free will, then they could choose between good and evil. And if they could choose sin and evil, they would surely die. And what could be done about the death of human beings when we created them to live forever? Well, the discussion didn't get very far so they tabled it for discussion at the next meeting.

Now that the minutes had been read they brought it back up again for discussion. Jesus starts the discussion by suggesting that he had some additional reflections. Jesus said that he realized that if human beings were given free will, then the Holy Spirit was very right—that human beings if they choose sin would surely die. Jesus said, "I've been thinking about this since the last meeting and I've decided that if they die, then I would be willing to go down and give my life that they might live again. If they choose sin and if they die, I will go and bring them back to life." The Holy Spirit wrote in the minutes—*The Lamb of God slain before the foundation of the world* (Rev.13:8). Jesus gave his life before the world began. He had already offered himself as a sacrifice before the creation of anything.

Now, let's fast forward. On the surface of things, he looked like a victim. He comes through forty and two generations; born on the backside of a cheap motel; goes around the earth making blind folk to see and deaf folk to hear, and the lame folk to walk. All of a sudden they got upset with him. He was arrested on false and trumped-up charges. He was taken from kangaroo court to kangaroo court. He was beaten, whipped, spat upon, and lied about. He was stripped of his clothing. They dressed him up in a fake purple kingly robe and made fun and sport of him: *Prophesy and tell us the name of the one who slapped you. You're supposed to be a prophet; tell us the name of the one who slapped you.* They mocked him. Put a crown of thorns on his head. They led him out to be rejected by the people that he had helped, and forced him to carry his cross in public shame and humiliation. Then they crucified him on a hill called Calvary. Jesus looks like a victim if there ever was a victim.

We have to remember that the plan had already been agreed upon before the foundation of the world. Jesus would go down and by the sacrifice of his life restore humankind. The Bible says that early on Sunday morning God brought Jesus up out of that grave, and he steps out and says, "All power is given in my hands on heaven and on earth." He is not a victim at all. It was the power of choice and the power of his generosity. He is not a victim. He says, "Nobody takes my life, I lay it down and pick it up when I want to." Jesus says, "I'm not a victim; I'm a victor!" I chose to lay my life down! I gave my life away. Generosity takes me out of being a victim!

Aren't you glad about it? God made you be a victor. God made you to live inside out. You are a not a victim; you are a victor. Nobody takes your life. You lay it down and pick it back up when you get ready.

THE BACKSTORY

In the attempt to dependably fulfill my responsibility as a pastor and church leader, I faithfully participated in seminars, workshops, and training sessions and read many books, articles, and essays on the subject of leadership. Most of them are concerned with how to teach certain habits that would make a leader more effective, such as time management, self-care, delegation, or vision casting. While these were important, my leadership effectiveness did not increase until my work with one of my major mentors, Edwin H. Friedman.[13] It was from Friedman that I began to understand the connection between leadership and maturity. Friedman taught

---

13. Edwin H. Friedman, *Generation to Generation: Family Process in Church and Synagogue* (New York: Guilford Press, 1985); *Friedman's Fables* (New York: Guildford Press, 1990); *A Failure of Nerve: Leadership in the Age of the Quick Fix* (New York: Seabury, 1997, posthumous).

that leadership had more to do with a leader's presence and being than with techniques and habits. Leadership had to do more with the emotional and spiritual maturity of the leader than the education and data available to the leader.

From Friedman I learned the devastating effects of victim thinking. Victim thinking was the opposite of the chief cornerstone of Friedman's work, self-differentiation (maturity). As I worked with the concept of self-differentiation, I became aware of how much victim thinking was in my life. I made a determined commitment to mature and to eradicate victim thinking. Also, following the work of W. Gary Gore, I began to espouse 100 percent responsibility as one of the core values of my life.[14] I had 100 percent responsibility for how I responded to the events in my life.

When I started my professional coach training with the Institute of Professional Excellence in Coaching (iPEC),[15] I had no idea how much victim thinking was still operative in my life. iPEC broadened the definition of victim to "being subject to something." To be a victim was to be subject to thoughts, beliefs, emotions, and perceptions that work against us, don't serve us well, or stop us from doing something that God would have us to do. By the time I started the training, I was being subject to powerlessness, hopelessness, and helplessness in my ministry context, but I could not name it. I was living as a victim as the senior pastor of the church.

One of the gifts that God has given me is preaching. Usually I preach with energy, passion, strength, confidence, insight, and clarity. Across the life of my ministry, the feedback consistently has been that I have been a high-quality preacher. All of a sudden, I noticed that my preaching was not uplifting and inspiring to me, and if not uplifting and inspiring to me, in all probability it was not to anyone else either. At first I thought it was a couple of off Sundays, and I rationalized that we cannot always preach our best sermons, but the same feeling persisted in me for several months. I thought that I was in a preaching slump, because my experience is that preachers, like hitters in professional baseball, can go

---

14. W. Gary Gore, *Navigating Change: A Field Guide to Personal Growth* (Memphis: Team Trek, 2002).

15. I grew so much personally and professionally by my experience in being coached by a coach from iPEC (Institute of Professional Excellence in Coaching) that I signed myself and my wife up for their coach training program. Both of us finished the coach training and are certified coaches. Many of the ideas in this book come from contact with the fresh ideas in the iPEC program. For more information contact www.ipeccoaching.com.

into a slump, and I thought that I would come out of it like hitters in baseball eventually come out of it. A year later, I was still in the slump.

I was not energetic in my preaching, but lethargic. I came to the awareness that I was subject to feelings and emotions that were outside of the pulpit that I brought to the pulpit with me. I was allowing what was going on outside the pulpit, my interpretation of it, and subsequently how I felt about it, to diminish my energy levels to the point of feeling helpless and hopeless in my preaching and leadership. I was a victim.

About this time, a friend gave me a book by Joan Chittister for my devotional reading.[16] At this point, I was sinking into depression, if I was not already there, and I asked God to help me make another choice about my interpretation and feelings. I read this paragraph from a chapter entitled "The Gift of Endurance," and the full extent of my victimhood hit me squarely in the face:

> There is a kind of pseudo-endurance, a neurosis of the spirit that warps our personalities and numbs our souls. We complain but we will not quit. We sulk but we do not change. We bear up but we do not enjoy. We miss the point entirely. We confuse endurance with sloth and drag our feet through life and expect the universe to thank us for the sacrifice we do not want to make. But endurance is not misery, not martyrdom, not spiritual masochism. Endurance means that I intend to survive the worst, singing as I go, and knowing as Jacob did [Gen 32], that I have seen the face of God and survived.[17]

I cried profusely after reading this. What Chittister described in this paragraph was exactly what was happening to me. I complained, but I would not quit. I sulked but would not make any substantive change. I bore the weight of ministry, but I did not enjoy it. And I did expect people to thank me for a sacrifice that I did not even want to make. I was in misery, martyrdom, and spiritual masochism. I was a victim to and subject to feelings of powerlessness, hopelessness, and helplessness, so much so that I could not operate out of one of my most gifted areas. I repented to God. I apologized to God, who had given me the gift of preaching,

---

16. Joan D. Chittister, *Scarred by Struggle, Transformed by Hope* (Grand Rapids: William B. Eerdman's, 2003).

17. Ibid., 77.

but because of my victim interpretation about life, I was neglecting my gift. I told God that I was wrong.

From that moment on, I determined to make a different choice. First, I said that I would never again allow anyone or anything, including myself, to block the free delivery of a gift that God gave me, namely preaching God's Word. I did not care what was happening or what was going on outside the pulpit or inside me. I was going to freely share my gift of preaching with energy, passion, strength, confidence, insight, and clarity. Second, in reading Matthew 5:38–42, I received the insight that generosity moves one out of the victim position and allows one to take control of one's life. I determined that I was going to be generous with my gifts in ministry and, if someone forced me to go one mile, I would go two miles. I was not a victim and, if someone took my outer cloak, I would give him/her my T-shirt as well. Nobody could take my gift, but I would make the choice to lay my life down. I would be generous with my gift in my preaching, and generosity would allow my gift to flow without hindrance. Realizing that the overwhelming majority of hindrances are internal, I determined to be unhindered in the pulpit.

Subsequently upon making the choice to be unhindered, I learned that when a God-given gift flows unhindered, and in generosity, the people who receive the gift are unusually blessed. The anointing of God flows through the gift around the room and the people experience themselves as unusually blessed by God. In response to my shift, the people experienced themselves as unusually blessed by God. And from the day I made this choice, I preached every sermon as though it were my last. I moved from victim to victory.

4

HAVE TO VS. WANT TO

Let us fix our eyes on Jesus, the author and perfecter of our faith,

who for the joy set before him endured the cross, scorning its

shame, and sat down at the right hand of the throne of God.

—HEBREWS 12:2 NIV

Have you ever been stuck? I don't mean stuck in the snow, or stuck on a project, stuck in your budget, or even stuck with a bill. I mean have you ever been stuck in your life? Have you ever felt like your whole life was stuck? Have you ever felt like you weren't making forward progress in your life? Your life was not going the way you wanted it to go, or where you wanted it to go. You were not accomplishing what you really wanted to accomplish. You were not making it happen like you really wanted to make it happen. Have you ever been stuck in life?

If you are not sure, there is one way that we can possibly measure whether or not our lives are stuck. There is one phrase that gives indication that our lives might be stuck. That one phrase is *I have to*. How many times we say *I have to* might indicate that our lives are stuck.

How many times do you say *I have to*? I have heard people say *I have to* many times. *I have to* go to work. *I have to* take care of these kids. *I have to* call my mother. *I have to* put up with these crazy folks on my job. *I have to* take the dog out. *I have to* do the laundry. We even say *I have to* go to church! And many of us say, *I have to* pray!

The phrase "have to" has to do with duty and responsibility. Duty and responsibility are important aspects of life. Duty and responsibility are necessary in getting things done and in helping society to function. Duty and responsibility can come from a sense of honor and privilege to serve and are critical to life and human community. For example, military personnel serve our country with a high sense of duty and responsibility, some even making the ultimate sacrifice. I think of duty and responsibility as values that allow breadwinners, male and female, to sacrifice and endure a competitive and sometimes mean world to put food on the table and a roof over the head of a family. Therefore, duty and responsibility are critical adhesives that hold society together.

However, there is a point when too much duty and responsibility move beyond service, privilege, and honor and become "have to." This is what I'm talking about—when duty and responsibility become a burden and a heavy load. When that is the case, we express it as "I have to." I have to take care of these kids. I have to pay these bills. I have to go to this job. I have to be bothered with this crazy sister! I have to! I have to! I have to!

Duty and responsibility under these circumstances mean that I'm forced to. It's not my true agenda, but I have to. I don't really have a choice. I would really rather be doing something else, but I have to. When we speak of "have to" in this manner, it leads to a certain kind of sacrifice, usually sacrifice without joy. When you sacrifice without joy, it leads to resentment. It leads to feelings of bitterness, anger, and antagonism. "I have to" can even lead to a downward spiral that is then expressed bitterly as: I hate this and I hate that, and I hate her and I hate him. Needless to say, this takes the fun out of living. If you're sacrificing, but you don't have joy in your sacrifice, then you say, I have to.

Ironically, we often think about what we have to do for others and we don't think much about what others think they have to do for us. We're not very good at being sensitive to what others have to do, to have to deal with us. For example, did my mother have to or did she want to? Was I a have to? Did my mother say, "I have to raise him," or "I have to cook for him" or was it "I want to"? Was I a *have to* or a *want to*?

Want to indicates there is joy and passion in doing. *Want to* is about duty and responsibility more in the direction of honor and privilege. *Want to* creates a desire to succeed and the feeling of ownership of one's own life. *Want to* is about the connection of who you are with what you're doing. If who you are is not connected with what you're doing, you're out of alignment. And when you're out of alignment, you use words like "have to" and "got to." When you are aligned, when who you are on the inside matches what you're doing on the outside, then you experience *want to*! And whenever you experience *want to*, it's a powerful motivation to succeed and a powerful means of owning your life!

"Want to" is about alignment of the core values of your inner self with your outer mission. If who you are at your core does not align with what you're doing in your everyday life, I don't care how much money you're making, it's a "have to"! I don't care how big the square footage of the house is, it's a "have to"! If you get a degree and it does not line up with who you are on the inside, it's a "have to"! And when you "have to," it's a burden, a weight, a responsibility. "Have to" ultimately ends in bitterness and resentment. It ends up with me saying, I hate my job; I hate my friends; I hate my life; I hate my home.

The derivative of "want to" is joy. When you want to, the life that you live is filled with joy! When you want to, it is an expression of who you really are to the outside world, and the expression is joy. You can sacrifice because the sacrifice is sustained by joy! Sacrifice is not sustained by bitterness, anger, and resentment. You can't sacrifice long and be healthy at the same time based on bitterness, resentment, and anger. The only thing that can sustain true sacrifice is joy.

I ask this question again: Was my mother bothered with me because she *had to* or because she *wanted to* be? Is my wife bothered with me because she has to or because she wants to be? Or another question—did Jesus have to be bothered with me or did he want to be? Our text says: *Let us fix our eyes on Jesus, the author and perfecter of our faith, who for the joy set before him endured the cross, scorning its shame, and sat down at the right hand of the throne of God (Heb. 12:2).* We are to run the race of life with our eyes fixed on Jesus. So, back to the relevant question: was securing our salvation a *have to* for Jesus or a want to for Jesus?

The text answers our question immediately, because wherever the word *joy* is, there's a *want to*. *Jesus is the author and perfecter of our faith, who for the joy set before him . . .* Jesus went to the cross because he wanted to.

Jesus went to the cross because of the joy that it would bring. He looked right through the cross to the coming joy for all humankind. The joy was his motivation! The joy was his inspiration, which means that the cross on the outside lined up with who he was on the inside! The value of duty, responsibility, honor, privilege, and love on the inside aligned with mission of the cross on the outside. Whenever who you are on the inside is aligned with what you are doing on the outside, joy is a byproduct!

Jesus went to the cross because of joy. How in the world could he experience joy knowing what the cross would be like? Everybody knows what the cross is. The cross is the crown of thorns on his head with blood streaming down; the open and torn flesh with the piercing in his side; the ring of the hammer as nails are driven in his hands and feet. The cross is bitter and unspeakable agony. What in the world could have that much joy such that, when you put it in comparison to the cross, the cross isn't even worth mentioning?

Jesus endured the cross and despised the shame. What could mean that much that he could endure the cross and despise the shame? Do you know what it means to despise the shame? It's to not be embarrassed by the embarrassment. That implies that the cross is embarrassing, but you have to choose to be embarrassed by the embarrassment. Nobody can embarrass you if you choose not to accept the embarrassment. He scorned the embarrassment. He scorned being made a fool out of. He pushed aside being rejected, being laughed at, being spat upon, being beaten, being whipped, and being crucified. What could have given him that much joy that he pushed all of this aside and said that it all was worth it? The text says, "who for the joy set before him endured the cross and despised the shame?" What could give that much joy?

Well, let me list a few things. How about his victorious resurrection? How about his victory over sin and hell? How about the conquering of death for all time? How about his glorious return to heaven, leading captivity captive? How about taking his place at the right hand of the Creator, who loves him without measure, and gave him the name that is above every name? How about the perfect fulfillment of the task that was set before him? When the text says, "who for the joy set before him . . ." it is indicating that Jesus' victorious resurrection, the conquering of death for all time, the glorious return to heaven, taking his place at the right hand of God who loves him beyond measure, and the perfect fulfillment of all he was given to do was nothing but pure unashamed, unadulterated, and unspeakable joy. And this joy diminished what the cross was all about.

"*. . . who for the joy set before him . . .*" The joy transformed a *have to* into a *want to*. Now, that makes my heart jump. All those reasons that I mentioned above are important, critical, and vital. But there is something that makes my heart jump even more than all of that. What in the world could make the heart jump more than conquering death for all time, a glorious return to heaven, or Jesus' taking his place at the right hand of God? What could make your heart jump more than the perfect fulfillment of all he had been given to do? The thing that makes my heart jump more than those just mentioned is the understanding that Jesus was thinking of me when he chose to follow the plan that had been set in motion before the foundation of the world. He was thinking of me. He was looking after me. He was taking care of me. He was mothering me. He was nurturing me. He was concerned about me. He loved and valued me so much that he counted all the pain, suffering, agony, and trauma as nothing! He counted it all as joy to receive me!

I get excited when I think about that because it helps me realize how much God loves me, how much God cares about me, and how precious I am in God's eyesight. And every time I realize how much God loves me, I realize that I am pretty enough, that I am good enough, and, it does not matter if they do not like me. And that gives me joy. He gives me joy because Jesus gives me a hope and a future. Jesus fills me with the Spirit of God and gives me everything I need for abundant life on the inside, starting with joy! And it makes me want to live life because I want to, not because I have to. I *want to* live; I *want to* serve; I *want to* love. I *want to* sacrifice.

I return to my previous question. Was I, for my mother, a "have to" or a "want to"? My mother used to get up early and get three kids ready for school. She would fix us breakfast and then drive us to school. She would drop us off at school and then drive to work. She would work eight hours and then drive back to pick us up. After picking us up, she'd come home and cook. Then she would try to make sure we got our homework done. I know all of that had to feel like she had to, but she made us feel like she wanted to. She made me feel like she wanted to do it. She made me feel like I was kind, like I was special, and she wanted to do it. She made me feel like I was smart. She made me feel like I had a future. She made me feel that I was on my way somewhere and she was doing everything she did so that I could walk into the future that God had for me. It was a "have to," but she made it feel like a "want to"!

If God uses me to bless people, it is because my mother made a "have to" feel like a "want to." If I sound intelligent, it is because my mother took a "have to" and made it feel like a "want to"! If I bless some people, my mother is in every word. My mother worked at Spiegel, a now closed catalog order house that was once on the south side of Chicago. She went to Wilson Junior College at night and matriculated to Chicago State University and got her degree to teach. My mother taught her first eighth grade class when I was in eighth grade. If my mother hadn't taught those eighth grade classes, I wouldn't have obtained the degrees that I have, gone the places that I have gone, and done the things that I have done. It's because my mother made it a "want to" rather than a "have to"!

Can anyone tell me that eating last is something someone wants to do? For a whole lot of mothers, when there is not enough food to go around, they eat less and last. You can tell me that's something they have to do, but Mama made it feel like she wanted to. You can't tell me dressing down when everybody's dressed up is something mothers want to do. We had a store in Chicago on 63rd Street called Robert Hall. Robert Hall was where you went for your Easter suits. It was a cheap store, but I thought it was Fifth Avenue when I was growing up. One year when Easter was drawing near, we didn't go to Robert Hall. Mother tried to explain that we couldn't go to Robert Hall this particular Easter. And because I was so concerned about me and had no sense of the big picture of what was really going on in life, I threw a temper tantrum because I couldn't go to Robert Hall. I ought to have a repentance service for all the dumb and stupid things that I said and the dumb and stupid stuff that we did, being self-absorbed, self-concerned, and worried about ourselves! Don't you know my mother wanted to take me to Robert Hall? Mother wore less so the rest of us could go to Robert Hall. And while we were all walking around with our Easter outfits, Mother had the same dress on. Don't tell me that was something she wanted to do! That was a "have to" that Mama made feel like a "want to"!

Jesus, for the joy set before him, made a "have to" into a "want to." It was for the moment that you and I received salvation and the moment you and I nurtured a relationship with the Lord Jesus Christ that he endured the cross and despised the shame. He makes a "have to" feel like a "want to."

Because of Christ, your life is about wanting to; it is not about having to. Your life is about joy; it's not about anger and resentment and bitterness. Go ahead and release the joy in your life. Go ahead and do what you want to do. You may have to save up for it, but go ahead and do what you want to do. Go ahead and align who you are on the inside with what you are doing on the outside. I'm not saying go to the job tomorrow and quit because you heard the pastor say, "This is a have to and I'm getting rid of all the have to's." What I'm saying is get a plan and work your plan. God will bring the day in your life where "have to" will become "want to," and you will come to know the joy that made the entire "have to" worth it.

This is the joy of being in a relationship with the Lord Jesus Christ. You have been made rich! I'm not talking about finance. I'm talking about who you are on the inside aligned up with what you're doing on the outside. You come to know unspeakable joy! You come to know the joy of doing what you've been called to do, the way you've been called to do it. There are some "have to's" in life, but if you live inside out, *have to* becomes *want to*. Thank God for my mother and thank God for Jesus, who took my life from a *have to* and made it become a *want to*.

THE BACKSTORY

In my work with iPEC, I learned the concept of "energetic engagement." While it is necessary to work with an iPEC coach or take the full training from iPEC to get a broader understanding of the concept, in this backstory section I present my interpretation of energetic engagement and how it helped me to live inside out.

In the backstory section from "The Power of Choice: I Choose," I discussed that our lives are shaped by our interpretations, and our interpretations are shaped by our consciousness, that is, our past and present thoughts, beliefs, behaviors, actions, and emotions. The concept of energetic engagement opened up key insights into my consciousness and gave me power of choice to shape the interpretations that form the character and contours of my life.

The first aspect of energetic engagement is the question: "Who am I?" When this question is asked, the assumption is that who we are is defined by what we value and what we believe. The formal definition of values is a tightly held belief (as opposed to a vague notion) upon which a person or organization acts by choice. For many of us, our values, and therefore who we are, is determined outside in. Our values are determined by our parents, media, culture, religious institutions, friends, and significant relationships. While none of us can know who we are without these critical participants in our lives, if they have too much influence and sway, then we live outside in. Because living outside in is not optimal living, it is important to live inside out, which is to choose our values and beliefs. Even when we choose the values and beliefs of our parents, religious institutions, or friends, it is our choice. By this choice, we take ownership and responsibility for our lives, and in no way are victims. This explanation is identified in Figure 1 in the circle to the left identified as "Who I am."

The second aspect of energetic engagement is: "What I do." This is my choice of profession, job, or how I choose to make a living in the world. We make the choice of job or profession based upon our values and who we believe that we are. If who we are is based on perspectives from the outside in, then we will find that what we do is also based upon that outside-in perspective. If we come to an understanding of ourselves from the inside out, then we choose what we do and determine how we make our living inside out. This explanation is identified in Figure 1 in the circle to the right, labeled "What I do."

The very bottom circle of Figure 1 explains the final and most important component of energetic engagement, "core energy." Core energy is the result of how much of my life is lived outside in versus inside out. The more inside out I live, the more positive core energy I have, and the more energetically engaged I am. The more energetically engaged I am, the more passion I possess about what I am doing. Therefore, core energy has to do with how an individual gets things done based upon his/her interest and passion. Core energy asks: What's a person's buy in? Does he/she want to do it or does she/he have to do it? Is he/she excited and enthused or does he/she feel forced? My energetic engagement is the interest, passion, desire, and enthusiasm, or lack thereof, to get something done. The lower circle entitled "Core Energy" depicts this explanation (See Figure 1).

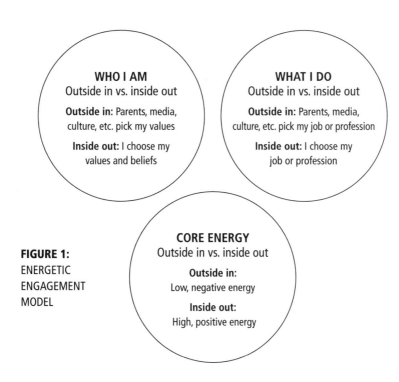

FIGURE 1:
ENERGETIC
ENGAGEMENT
MODEL

When a person's core energy is low, such as when he/she uses the language "have to," it usually means that there is a lack of alignment between "Who I am" and "What I do." In most cases, it starts in the "Who I am" being based on outside in rather than inside out. In my particular case, my "Who I am" was outside in and based upon a combination of influences from family and culture. I came to believe outside in that I was to be a martyr, and I was to be nice. As I was reflecting on my "Who I am," a story surfaced that shows me adopting the role of martyr and being nice (See Figure 2).

In my third grade class, while the teacher was writing on the board with her back turned to the class, someone threw a paper airplane and it almost hit her and came crashing down at her feet off the board. The whole class burst into suppressed and muffled laughter. She was infuriated and said that no one was going anywhere until the class revealed who threw the airplane. The class did not move and no one offered up a name, and so she waited and waited and waited. Well, still no one offered a name.

At the end of the day, I came to a resolution of the impasse. I admitted that I threw the airplane. She immediately let the entire class go home and held me after class. She said that this kind of behavior was unusual for me, and asked me why I had done it. After interrogation, I confessed that I had not done it, but I said that I had done it so that everyone could go home. She was flustered and said that I would receive the punishment just the same. What was it that made me offer myself up as a sacrifice for the class? How did I decide in third grade that I was to be sacrificial and I was to be nice? How did these come to be my values at such an early age?

Let me move to the second circle, "What I do." Later on in life, based upon the values of martyrdom and niceness, I chose a profession that, from my perspective, required me to be a martyr and to be nice—pastoral ministry and helping people. Allow me to relate a very important story that led to my choice of profession, which allowed me to be a martyr and nice.

In the last year of seminary, I took a class at the Catholic seminary. My seminary was in a cluster of seven theological schools, and we could take classes at any school and it would apply to our degree at our home seminary. I decided to take an Old Testament class on the Hebrew prophets taught by Professor Carroll Stuhlmueller. Professor Stuhlmueller taught from the perspective of the very best of intellectual scholarship and the very best of heart and belief in the faith. It was a pleasure for me to come to class every week because I knew that he believed the Bible.

Somewhere in the semester, he assigned a paper on Amos 5:24—let justice roll down like waters and righteousness like a mighty stream. I wrote the paper and turned it in at the appointed hour. The next week, Professor Stuhlmueller asked if there was a Frank Thomas in class. With nervousness, I raised my hand. He said that he wanted to see me after class. After class, he invited me to his office. I walked in and immediately felt that I was in a holy place. When I sat down, he asked: "What are you going to do with your ministerial life?" I responded that I was on my way to a PhD program. My plan was to spend my life teaching. He graciously said to me that the world had enough teachers and what was needed were pastors. He remarked how impressed he was with the great sensitivity with which I treated the Amos 5:24 text. I remarked that I had no plans to pastor. I had watched how the pastor in my field internship had been treated by several leaders in the congregation, and I wanted no part of the bitter and painful life of church conflict. I remember saying to him, "Church folks are crazy." He was insistent that I had gifts for pastoring. People needed my sensitivity and insight into the text. He would not relent, so I got out of there as fast as I could.

Until this meeting with Professor Stuhlmueller, I was dead set against pastoring. I had seen too much of church wars, and I did not want to be involved. I left there with the fact that an authority figure said that I had gifts, and something opened up in me, the potential and possibility of pastoring. Based upon my discussion with Professor Stuhlmueller, I put my teaching plans on hold and became a pastor. Other than Dr. Stuhlmueller, and the Holy Spirit of God, I know that it also had to do with the role of being a martyr and being nice. Pastors were people who were sacrificial and nice. I chose the profession based upon who I believed myself to be.

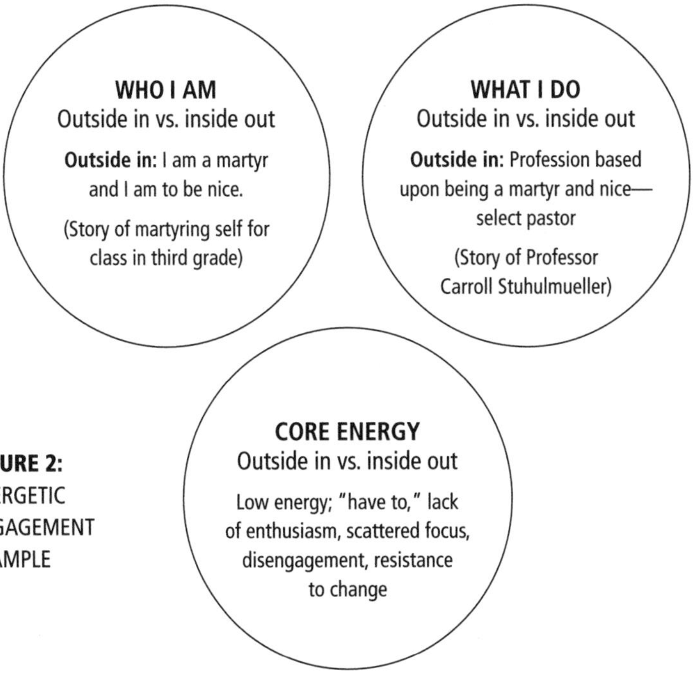

WHO I AM
Outside in vs. inside out

Outside in: I am a martyr and I am to be nice.

(Story of martyring self for class in third grade)

WHAT I DO
Outside in vs. inside out

Outside in: Profession based upon being a martyr and nice—select pastor

(Story of Professor Carroll Stuhulmueller)

CORE ENERGY
Outside in vs. inside out

Low energy; "have to," lack of enthusiasm, scattered focus, disengagement, resistance to change

FIGURE 2:
ENERGETIC
ENGAGEMENT
EXAMPLE

What I can attest to, in terms of the third box, core energy, is that after thirty-one years of pastoral ministry, I experienced low energy, including a lack of enthusiasm, scattered focus, disengagement, and resistance to change (See Figure 2). Ministry had the feeling of "have to." Many nights in the quietness of the prayer of my soul, I admitted to God and myself that I did not really love doing this (pastoral ministry). Based upon who I understood myself to be, and the profession that I chose as a result of who I understood myself to be, I believed that I had to pastor because I had to be a martyr and I had to be nice. I was out of alignment: who I really am did not line up with what I was doing, and the result was lack of energy at my core. My energetic engagement was very low. I was engaged by default. Upon explaining this to one of my friends, he suggested that I was tired and needed a sabbatical. Instantly, from the inside out came this comment: if I took a sabbatical, I would not come back. My life as a senior pastor, other than preaching and a few other places of service was a "have to."

I prayed earnestly and feverishly to God to help me turn my "have to" into a "want to." Let's now turn to the next phase in the journey to inside out, "Defining the Choice."

part two

DEFINING THE CHOICE

✦ 5 ✦

AS ONE WITH AUTHORITY

They went to Capernaum, and when the Sabbath came, Jesus
went into the synagogue and began to teach. The people were
amazed at his teaching because he taught them as one who had
authority, not as the teachers of the law.

—MARK 1:21–22 NIV

Each and every time I get ready to do something great for the Lord, or to step out in a new area of risk for the Lord, or to move out of my comfort zone for the Lord, or really become bold and courageous for the Lord, the enemy will stop me and ask me a specific question: "By what authority do you do this? By what authority do you do these things and who gave you the authority that you believe you have? By what authority do you believe that you can have a God-given vision for your life and you can act and fulfill that vision?" This text says that Jesus taught as one with authority. He didn't teach as the scribes of the law, but he taught as one with authority.

Jesus came to the temple on the Sabbath and taught. And, when he taught, the people were amazed at his teaching and said, "He teaches as one with authority." They remarked that his teaching was substantially different from that of the teachers of the law. His teaching had authority. What did Mark and the people mean? Was it his communication and homiletical style that impressed them such that they said he taught with authority? Was Jesus a lecturer in a quiet reserved manner, or was Jesus a whooper who brought his organist to worship, and the people were impressed with his musical and celebrative close? Did Jesus have humor in his presentation? Was it humor that made them feel and connect with the message so that they could say, "This one teaches as no one has ever taught before"? Was Jesus inductive or deductive? Was he expository or narrative? Did Jesus use three points and a poem? What was Jesus' teaching style? What made him effective as a teacher?

I believe that when they said he taught with authority, they saw and felt in Jesus' teaching something deeper than style or form of the message. You can have humor, but no authority. You can be a whooper with no authority. You can be a teacher, but have no authority. You can be expository or narrative and have no authority. It's something deeper than just a teaching style that made Jesus stand out among the people. The people summarized it as authority.

Many of us like the word *authority* because of its relationship to the word *power*. In a world of shrinking resources, we want power, which gives us control, because power and control will guarantee that we get at least our share of resources. We are, as human beings, very interested in and attentive to who has power and who is in relationship with those who have power, because power or a relationship with power means access to life's resources. We like to be with those who have power over things: power to maneuver a person or a place to an outcome that is pleasurable or that we like, power to have dominion over—preeminence, superiority, and authority over. We often think that power means having the ability to distribute and use our power for our self-interests.

However, I suggest to you that Mark means something different by "authority." I want to suggest an alternative to what the world traditionally considers as "power." What I am more interested in is to redefine "authority," from "power over" to "power within." I want to talk about authority as the power and determination within myself to do what God says to do without the normal internal blocks and excuses that steer me away from what I know God would have me to do.

Ultimately, what I am suggesting is nobody blocks us from our God-given destiny but us. What I'm suggesting is that nobody can stop us but us. We stop ourselves. We block ourselves on the inside. We have doubt and uncertainty. We are fearful that we are not good enough to really do what God would have us to do. We ask: am I smart enough to really be what God would have me to be? We have excuses and human blocks, and so the power is blocked on the inside. And when the power is blocked on the inside, it cannot flow to the outside. With Jesus, the power flowed inside out, and that is why the people could say that he taught as one with authority. With Jesus, the power of his teaching flowed inside out. The real work of life is to live inside out.

When we live inside out, we must answer two profound questions: what do I know to be true and what do I want, really. First, what do I know at the core of my being to be true? What do I know in the bottom of my soul, at the very core of me, to be true? Not just what I say is true, but what I live as truth. The world is filled with much spoken truth, but I am talking about the truth that we live. What do I know beyond any shadow of a doubt to be true? I often give this example to explain what I mean by this question: I go to the doctor's office and the doctor tells me that tests indicate that I have cancer. Upon receiving the news, I have to interpret it and give the news meaning. Ultimately, I interpret the news based upon what I know to be true at my inner core. What I know to be true is what I tell myself to be able to get up and walk out of that office sane. What I know to be true is what I tell myself to give myself courage to live and not die. Now, some people do receive the news as a death sentence. Some people see it as a life sentence. It all depends on what you tell yourself in your inner core, what you know to be true. This is the level of truth that I am espousing in the question "what do you know to be true?" It is the truth that makes sense of life in our most tragic or triumphal moments. What did Jesus know to be true?

Mark opens his Gospel by proclaiming the good news that Jesus is the Messiah, the son of God. Prophecy foretold that when the Messiah came, a messenger, Elijah, would come before the Messiah to prepare the way. Mark introduces us to John the Baptist, the forerunner of Jesus. John appeared in the wilderness, baptizing for the repentance of sin and announcing that another was coming whose sandals he was not worthy to stoop down and untie. John baptizes with water, but the one who comes after baptizes with the Holy Spirit. Jesus comes to meet John and is baptized by John, and, as Jesus comes out of the water, verse 11 of the text says that a voice from heaven proclaims, "You are my Son, whom I love; with you I am well pleased." As Jesus comes out of the water, and after divine affirmation, at once the Spirit drives him into the wilderness for forty days to be tempted by Satan.

I believe that after his affirmation from heaven, it was necessary to go into the wilderness to be tempted so he would be forced to define and refine what he believed was true. Jesus was getting ready to do something big for God and Satan had to challenge him and ask him, "By what authority?" The wilderness was the solitary and the lonely place, where he met challenges from Satan to his heaven-given authority, and we are told the angels attended to him. We know that the angels attended him because of the fierceness of his struggle with Satan. He comes out the wilderness clear and focused, knowing what he believes to be true at the core of his being—having authority.

In Mark 1:14–15, after John the Baptist was put in prison, Jesus went into Galilee proclaiming the good news of God. Jesus announced that the reign of God was here. At the core of his very being and existence, Jesus believed that the reign of God was true. Jesus has answered the first question. Jesus knew the reign of God was true.

The second question is "What do I want, really?" What I want, really, flows out of what I know to be true. Many of us know what we want. Based on living outside in or living according to the flesh, I would like to be rich, famous, and powerful and have more money than I could ever spend. That is what I want, but is that what I want, really? What I want, really, gets at what I am after in wanting what I want. What am I really after in wanting to be rich, famous, or powerful? Let's say that I am really after affirmation of my value and worth and these outside factors such as money, wealth, and power demonstrate to me my clear value and worth. What we want is money, wealth, and power. What we want, *really*, is to be valued. There is a difference between what I want, and what I want, really. What we want, really, is intricately connected to what we know to be true because, ultimately, we want what is true. What did Jesus want, really?

We know that the reign of God was true for Jesus. With the reign of God being really true, what did Jesus want, really? The answer is implied in his actions in Mark 1:14–15—he proclaimed the good news of God. He wanted people to repent and believe the good news. He wanted people to accept the good news and live according to the reign of God. What did Jesus really want?—to proclaim the message of the good news so that people would believe the reign of God and change their lives. That is what Jesus wanted, really.

When you know what you believe to be true and you know what you want, really, you discover your deepest passion. Jesus had a profound passion to share the reign of God with the world. When you have intense passion, you are willing to put your life on the line to see what you believe happen. All of a sudden, you discover that there is no one blocking you. You discover that happiness is not dependent on other people, or as Edwin H. Friedman would say, "Your salvation is not dependent on the functioning of other people."[18] You live out your Christian life to the best of your ability and you are not concerned with obtaining approval from others. It is then that you attain inner authority. You come to discover in the truest sense that all limits are internal.

This is why Jesus' teaching sounded different. This is why Jesus felt different. The only way the people hearing him could describe him was, *"He carries himself like one with authority!"* It was not simply a matter of style and form but a matter of belief and conviction. It was not a matter of using humor in the message, though Jesus used humor; it was a matter of being clear about what Jesus knew to be true and what he wanted, really. It was about his great passion for the reign of God. His passion made him teach differently, made him sound different.

Now that we are clear about Jesus' authority, what about your authority? What do you know to be true? And how does what you know to be true intertwine with what you want, really? What kind of authority do you have in your life? First, if you don't know what is true, then you do not know what you want, really, which means that your life does not flow

---

18. Edwin H. Friedman, seminar, "The Center for Family Process," October 1993, personal notes.

from you inner core, which means that you do not have authority. There-fore, when you sing, you sing like the teachers of the law. You don't have authority. When you preach, you preach like the teachers of the law. You don't have authority. Jesus was crystal clear about what he knew to be true. He was also crystal clear about what he wanted. Being crystal clear about what he knew and what he wanted, really, gave him authority!

What do you want, really? I assume that you want what is true! I be-lieve that it takes a tremendous amount of prayer and reflection to come to know what you know to be true and to come to know what you want, really. You can't answer these kinds of questions quickly and easily. You've got to get before God and have prayer and meditation and ask yourself these questions. You've got to go through some trials and some tribulations to discover what you really believe. And, until you know what you believe and you know what's true, you don't know what you really want! And so, you don't have any authority. The real work is acting on, doing, what you believe, and when you do what you believe, you are exercising inner authority. It's inside out—not outside in. Can I tell you what I know to be true? I believe that Jesus Christ is the Savior of the world and, based upon his resurrection, evil is defeated. I believe the gospel of Jesus Christ is good news for the world. Now that I have told you what is true, can I tell you what I want, really? I want to please God. I want to live a life that is pleasing to God. I want to do the right things in all relationships. And because I want to please God, I follow and exe-cute the teachings of Jesus Christ.

THE BACKSTORY

While it was very difficult to admit, in truth, the root of this sermon is that I had lost the sense of my own inner authority. One of the major struggles in my life is this question of authority, and I was fascinated that Jesus so fully lived out of his inner authority. I wondered what the source of his authority was. My inner au-thority was too much outside in, which resulted in people-pleasing behavior, seek-ing approval from others, and avoidance of conflict.

While in iPEC coach training, I underwent coaching myself. Not only did I get coaching from my peers in the program, but I engaged one of the lead trainers for coaching because I believed the training presented an opportunity for significant change in my life.[19] This fine and outstanding coach was instrumental in asking me key open-ended questions, and she used a stick man diagram to unlock several key insights, which in turn helped me locate my authority inside out.

After this question of my inner authority surfaced in a particularly moving coaching session, she asked me to get out a piece of paper and draw a stick man. I drew an ordinary stick man. She instructed me to draw a square box right above the point where the two legs intersected. She explained that this square box was my gut and my inner core. It was the center of my life containing my beliefs, thoughts, emotions, reflections, and experiences, which she summed up as the totality of my consciousness. In this place, at my inner core, resided what I believed to be true. She then instructed me to find the place where the arms intersected with the head, and right below that spot to draw a heart. She said that only when we know what is true do we come to know what we want, really. I did exactly as the coach asked.

When my drawing was complete, the coach then asked me if I was ready to respond to two questions: what did I know to be true at my inner core, and what did I want, really? I indicated to her that I needed some time to pray and reflect about these questions because I wanted to be honest and truthful with myself. One week later, in our next session, I gave her my responses: I know God sent Jesus Christ to be the Savior of the world, and what I want, really, is to please God, proclaim the good news of Jesus Christ, and do the right thing in all relationships. The coach asked me how my responses felt. I said they felt inside out.

The coach said to me that once I knew what I want, really, then my passion would become clear to me. The coach then asked, "Given what you know is true and what you want, really, what is your passion?" I said, without hesitation, "To preach and teach the gospel of Jesus Christ in creative and relevant sermonic forms that offer people hope for their lives." My response was instant and without hesitation because I once wrote this as the mission statement for my life. I knew it inside out and, when I was presented with that open-ended question, it popped up quickly and naturally.

---

19. Barb Heenan is a lead trainer at the Institute for Professional Excellence in Coaching (iPEC), a professional certified coach (PCC), and a member of the International Coaching Federation (ICC). She has her own coaching practice, Fresh Company Coaching and Consulting, http://www.freshcompanycc.com/. Barb is the creator of the stick man exercise. There are even more layers and insights involved; I just, for the sake of simplicity, scratched the surface with it.

Next, she told me that from passion flows the joy of vocation. When our inner passion meets a deep need in the exterior world, we discover the joy of a vocation, or what many of us know as a call. The coach asked me to draw hands on my stick man and then feet. The coach explained the hands and feet were how we were to implement the call; it was the work that our hands and feet were to do in the world. She asked, "What is your call?" I said two things: (1) Preach in creative and relevant sermonic forms and teach the same to others and (2) coach preachers, pastors, and others who want to live inside out (more about this later). One week later, after much reflection, I sharpened the call question to this (which I said earlier in the introduction):

> After much prayer, it is clear to me that in the closing years of my ministry, it is my life's work now to develop, mentor, encourage, inspire, and do whatever is necessary to cultivate a cadre of scribes and scholars, African American and otherwise, who are committed to transforming the world through sharing the genius of the African American preaching tradition.

The coach then asked, "What must you do to follow the call?" I told her, "I would have to re-create my entire life." She asked me what re-creation of my entire life would mean. I said that I would retire from the role of senior pastor. Even though I had spoken this out loud for the first time, I felt no sense of panic or anxiety. As a matter of fact, I felt absolutely calm. I was speaking inside out. What I had said needed no outside approval. I was not concerned with pleasing anyone, except God. That decision was made from my own inner authority.

As I was reflecting upon the truth uttered in that session, namely, that I would retire from the role of senior pastor, it became clear that I needed a plan. Retiring would significantly affect my family, my church family, and the community. I would have to carefully and thoughtfully construct a plan. I moved on in the coaching sessions to develop the plan.

6

AMAZING GRACE: BLIND BUT NOW I SEE

A second time they summoned the man who had been blind.
"Give glory to God by telling the truth," they said. "We know
this man is a sinner." He replied, "Whether he is a sinner or not,
I don't know. One thing I do know. I was blind but now I see!"

—JOHN 9:24–25 NIV, PARAPHRASED

This text brings into bold view the reality of blindness and seeing: some are blind, and yet they see, and some see and yet they are blind. What I want to suggest is that seeing has to do with believing, and if you do not believe, then you do not see. Some would suggest that you see first, and then you believe. I want to argue that we believe first, and then we see. We see what we believe. And if we are not careful, we will only see what we already believe, which will leave us narrow-minded, rigid, inflexible, and unyielding. If what we believe cannot change, then what we see cannot change, and therefore, as this text so clearly illustrates, we are blind. The human condition is that more often than not we are blind, not because we do not see, but because it is so very difficult for us to change what we believe.

Jesus intervenes in the situation of this blind man in John 9. He puts mud on his eyes. The man washes in the pool, and then he can see. You would think that this would be a time of victory and celebration, but this is the point when the real trouble begins. After the miracle, the neighbors are so surprised that the man can see that they begin to debate as to whether or not it is really him. They ask, "Is this the one who was blind and went around begging?" Some said, "Yes," and some said, "No." Several of them said, "But it looks just like him." He kept saying to them, "I am the man." They asked for details, "Who healed you and what happened?" He told them exactly what happened. They asked where Jesus was, and he said that he did not know.

Then the neighbors took the man to the Pharisees. Now, the first problem that the Pharisees had was that Jesus healed the man on the wrong day—the Sabbath. We notice that they are blind already in that what they believe will not let them see a miracle. They make a big deal about the day and disbelieve the healing. They interrogate the man, and he tells them that Jesus took mud and smoothed it over his eyes, and when it was washed away he could see. Some of them said that Jesus could not be from God because he healed on the wrong day. Others said, "But how can anyone do these signs?" There was deep division among them. The Pharisees again questioned the man: "Who do you think that he is?" The man replied, "I think that he must be a prophet."

The Jewish leaders would not believe that this man had been born blind, so they called his parents. They asked them, "Is this your son? Was he born blind? How is it that he can see?" They verify that this is their son and that he was born blind. They did not know how he could see or who healed him. The parents said, "He is of age, ask him." They were afraid of the Jewish leaders, who had announced that anyone saying Jesus was the Messiah would be expelled from the synagogue.

So for the second time, the leaders called the man in and said, "Tell the truth, because we know that Jesus is a sinner." Again, you see what you believe. The man says, "I do not know whether or not he is a sinner, but what I do know is that I once was blind but now I see." That should have settled the matter, but they still asked, "What did he do? How did he heal you?" The man said, "I told you once. Didn't you listen? Why do you want to hear it again? Do you want to be one of his disciples too?" They cursed him and said, "You are one of his disciples, but we are disciples of Moses. We know God spoke to Moses, but as for this man, we don't know anything about him." The man said "That's strange—he healed me, and you say that you do not know anything about him? If this man were not from God, he would not be able to do it." They said, "You were born in sin and you are trying to teach us?" And they threw him out of the synagogue.

The blindness of the man born blind represents all of us in our human condition. We are born blind. We enter the world and are indoctrinated into beliefs and systems of thought, whether in our families or in the cultural, religious, political, economic, and social systems. These systems in which we believe shape what we see, how we see, and when we see. Jesus has to put mud on our eyes and we wash so that we can see.

The blindness of the Pharisees is human blindness based on limiting beliefs, inaccurate assumptions, and false interpretations. They did not believe so they could not see. They believed that Jesus healed on the wrong day—that was their limiting belief; that belief about the prohibition of healing on the Sabbath limited their ability to see anything other than their narrow interpretation of the Law. They could not see a healing. Then, they followed with an inaccurate assumption: Jesus must be a sinner. If he heals on the wrong day, he is a sinner. Then they made a false interpretation: he cannot be from God. And even when confronted with the testimony of a blind man who was healed, when confronted with eyewitness testimony, the evidence standing right in front of them, because of what they believed, they could not see.

This human blindness is also a part of our economic system. Our nation believes that capitalism is the best economic system that the world has ever seen and any evidence to the contrary we cannot see. We cannot see that, under capitalism, regardless of how the economy expands, it cannot and will not eradicate poverty. And so we do not even really see, and therefore are blind to poverty in this country.

Beyond that, many are blind in relationships—blind to the fact of the deep love of our families for us while many of us as clergy run around ministering to the needs of everyone but them. Many of us are blind to true love and intimacy offered to us; blind to deep caring by another human being; blind to the demands of justice and equality; blind to the wide distribution of wealth between the rich and the poor; blind to anyone and anything outside of the interests of our little group; and especially blind to our own faults and shortcomings. We are as blind as the Pharisees in this text.

At the deepest level, this text is about whether our belief systems can handle new revelation, about whether we believe that God is done revealing, or if God continues to reveal in the present. If we believe that God is still revealing, then can what we believed in the past be amended, adapted, updated, and adjusted based on new revelation? Are we open to new revelation? Can we change what we believe so that we can change what we see?

Because we are blind, Jesus comes into our lives and puts mud on our eyes; he tells us to go and wash in the pool of Siloam, and when we wash the mud off of our eyes we can see. Have you ever been touched by God with a revelation and that revelation changed what you believed? Based on a new revelation, have you ever stood flat footed and just plainly told God that you were wrong? I do not mean wrong for small sins and small infractions, for insensitive actions or impure thoughts. But I mean, have you ever told God that you were wrong at the level of belief? Have you ever told God that you were wrong about what you believed? Have you ever owned up to the fact that what you believed would not allow you to see, and when presented with new revelation, you resisted because you would have had to change what you believed, and it is very hard to change what you believe? Have you ever told God that you were wrong at the level of belief?

Can I get to the heart of it now? Have you ever admitted to God that you were wrong because what you initially believed was rooted in fear? I am suggesting that underneath our ability to change what we believe is fear. If a miracle is standing right in front of you, like the blind man who now could see, and we cannot change what we believe, then our belief is based in fear. I was helped immensely to name fear and fear-based belief by a poem entitled "Gremlin Poem" by Lou Tice. Here is an excerpt:

I am Fear.
I am the menace that lurks in the paths of life, never visible
to the eye but sharply felt in the heart.
I am the father of despair, the brother of procrastination, the
enemy of progress, the tool of tyranny.

Born of ignorance and nursed on misguided thought, I have
darkened more hopes, stifled more ambitions, shattered
more ideals and prevented more accomplishments than
history could record.

Like the changing chameleon, I assume many disguises.
I masquerade as caution.
I am sometimes known as doubt or worry.
But whatever I'm called, I am still fear, the obstacle of
achievement.[20]

My blindness is really fear. My blindness is that my beliefs are based
in fear. I am afraid of change, afraid of being different, afraid that I have
been wrong all this time. The voice of fear reminds me that I am inadequate; I am not smart enough; I am defective and cannot be fixed. And
because of this fear, I have been clinging to my belief, and it cannot
change because I am not sure of who I might become.

Once we face the fear, and once we name the fear, once we unmask it,
it can be confronted and overcome. And once you confront the fear, you
know the joy of being able to see. The joy is that once you tell God you were
wrong about what you believed, then the mud on your eyes opens you to
see your fear, and once you see your fear, you can really see. When I confront
my fear, I can change what I believe, and when I change what I believe, then
I can see. When I admit to God that I am wrong, then it dismisses the fear.
When I tell God I am wrong, I can see. Once I was blind, but now I see.

When I told God I was wrong, I woke up one morning and saw my
wife for the very first time: saw how much she loved me and how much
she cared for me and saw how much I cared for and loved her. I woke up
and saw the poor and saw that I was one of them, and all of my middle-
class striving was not for my own security, but for the purpose of helping
people. I woke up one morning and saw that our nation needed fundamental change and so did the church. I woke up one day and realized
that I have fewer years left than the ones that have gone by and, in fact,

20. Lou Tice, "I Am Fear," http://portmacquarie-counselling.blogspot.com/2010/11/i-am-
fear.html, accessed 12/20/12.

that I was going to die and I had better appreciate every moment. I was blind to how fragile life is, but now I see. When I told God I was wrong, I woke up one day and was more fully human, more humane, more compassionate and loving like Jesus. I discovered that I was less judgmental and more merciful. I was more open to intimacy that was being offered to me. I could see. And all I could say was, "Amazing Grace!" And I was able to say with the songwriter: "Amazing grace, how sweet the sound that saved a wretch like me; I once was lost, but now am found, was blind but now I see."

THE BACKSTORY

In the backstory of the sermon "From Victim to Victory!" I went into great detail about my preaching slump and about repenting to God and telling God that I was wrong. I want to tell of that experience in more depth and give the reader a more thorough explanation of what I mean when I talk about admitting to God I was wrong. When it came to my own inner authority, I operated in fear. This fear manifested itself in a need for the approval of people, and I allowed the need for the approval of people to hinder the full operation of my gift of preaching and my leadership as well.

Again, it started in a coaching session. I made a comment in frustration, and it revealed a limiting belief. I said that I could not stop people from secret meetings. I lived with the reality that people would say one thing in a meeting, but after the meeting, people would have the "real" meeting in the parking lot or on the phone lines. People would say one thing in the meeting, and then do something completely different outside of the meeting. People would even orchestrate group-think ahead of and after the meeting.

The coach challenged me about my limiting belief and asked me this painful question: how might my leadership style contribute to secret meetings? The coach asked for permission to explain the question. Reluctantly, I agreed and continued the discussion despite feeling defensive and suspecting that the coach was trying to blame the secret meetings on me. The coach explained that if a leader is unclear about his/her vision and boundaries, then the leader sends mixed messages. When a leader sends mixed messages, the leader is not clear about how he/she wants to be treated. She said leaders tend to create the environment that a leader operates in. The coach knew of my struggle with authority and my need to seek approval of others and she pointed out that if a leader is oversensitive to the feelings of others, the leader sends mixed messages that create in-fighting. If I am not able or willing to stand up for myself and say things that are uncomfortable, I have contributed to secret meetings. She labeled this kind of leadership as "waffling."

Subsequently, after reflection about the conversation, I diagrammed what I heard the coach say about leadership in Figure 3:

FIGURE 3: BUILDING MY LIFE FROM THE INSIDE OUT: THE REPENTANCE

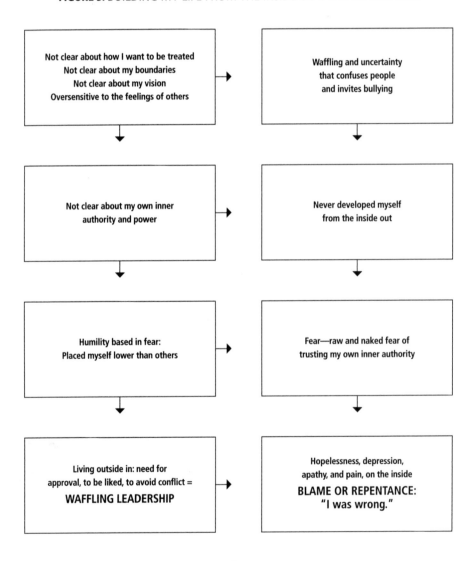

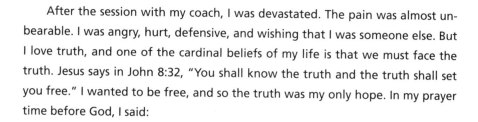

After the session with my coach, I was devastated. The pain was almost unbearable. I was angry, hurt, defensive, and wishing that I was someone else. But I love truth, and one of the cardinal beliefs of my life is that we must face the truth. Jesus says in John 8:32, "You shall know the truth and the truth shall set you free." I wanted to be free, and so the truth was my only hope. In my prayer time before God, I said:

> I accept and surrender to this truth. I take full responsibility for my lack of authority. I admit to you, God, that I have been wrong. I have been wrong at the level of belief about my authority. What I believed about my own authority was based in fear, and I repent before you. I need your help to make change in my life.

When I repented before God, many insights poured in from my inner authority. When I do not stand up for myself and say things that are uncomfortable, I allow people to have inappropriate power by denying my own power. This lack of confidence in my inner authority has been masked as humility. Humility will not serve me or anyone else if I do not see my own value. Humility does not mean that I humble myself below the level of other people. Humility is to value myself equally with other people. I created a paradigm for myself that did not allow me to express the depths of my own inner authority and power. I needed the help of God and my coach to redirect my life to live out of my own inner authority, that is, inside out.

I spent several days in the attitude and disposition of repentance before God for my own blindness. Even in the position of repentance, I was able to say, "Amazing grace, how sweet the sound that saved a wretch like me; I once was lost, but now am found, was blind but now I see."

7

A BASIN, A WATER PITCHER, AND A TOWEL

*Jesus knew that the Father had put all things under his power,
and that he had come from God and was returning to God; so
he got up from the meal, took off his outer clothing, and wrapped
a towel around his waist. After that, he poured water into a
basin and began to wash his disciples' feet, drying them with the
towel that was wrapped around him.* —JOHN 13:3–5 NIV

There sat at the entrance to the door a basin, a water pitcher, and a towel—all used for the washing of the feet of the guests as they entered a home after travel on the dank, dusty, and dangerous Palestinian roads—a basin, a water pitcher, and a towel. It was the sign of generous hospitality. Washing feet was what servants did; only servants used the basin, the water pitcher, and the towel as they washed and dried dirty feet. Washing feet was reserved for those of the lowest status and position in the culture; it was reserved for those who had no claim to dignity, worth, value, or honor that anybody was bound to respect. Only those of little value and worth used the basin, the water pitcher, and the towel.

There sat at the entrance to the door a basin, a water pitcher, and a towel as the disciples came into the home. They did not see anyone to handle the basin, the water pitcher, and the towel. There were no servants in their midst, or so they thought, so they gave up on having their feet washed. They all passed the basin, the water pitcher, and the towel. It was not their task. It was not their duty. It was not their responsibility. In some ways, it was beneath them. They were not servants. They were more interested in being served, and so as they entered the home, the basin, the water pitcher, and the towel sat there.

There sat at the entrance to the door a basin, a water pitcher, and a towel as Jesus entered the room. He saw them there, and important things were going on in his mind. The text says in verse 1 that it was right before the Passover meal. Jesus knew that the time had come for him to leave this world and go back to God. His leaving and his purpose were on his mind, so he looked and saw the basin, the water pitcher, and the towel. The text says that he loved his own who were in the world, but it was time to go, and since it was time to go, it was time to show the full extent of his love. He loved his disciples to the very end as he noticed the basin, the water pitcher, and the towel. There sat by the door a basin, a water pitcher, and a towel as the evening meal was in progress.

The devil had already prompted Judas Iscariot to betray Jesus, and so we know that these are the last moments and the arrest and crucifixion are at hand. Despite the atmosphere dripping with death, the text sets up a contrast between the power of Jesus and the basin, the water pitcher, and the towel. The text in verse 3 says Jesus knew that God had put all things under his power. Do not miss the contrast that the writer is setting up here. Jesus knew that he had the power in any and every situation. God had put all things under his power. No matter the situation and circumstance, Jesus was the power. He had the control. He had the command, the authority, the clout, the supremacy, the influence, the muscle, the sway, the swag, the juice, the ice, the rock—all power was already in his hands. Do you know how people would act if they had all power? They would not do what he was about to do with the basin, the water pitcher, and the towel.

Verse 3 continues: Jesus knew that he had come from God and that he was going back to God. He knew that he was of another world. No matter what happened in this world, he was not from this world and was not subject to the dictates, conditions, and circumstances of this world. The Prince of the Air runs this world, but since Jesus was not of this world, the Prince of the Air did not run him. He saw the basin, the water pitcher, and the towel.

Now, with all that knowledge, all that power, and all that confidence, you would expect that he would give orders. You would expect that he would reign, rule, and super-rule. You would expect a coronation and an enthronement; you would expect throngs of thousands and ten thousands willing to do his bidding and every command. You would expect entourages, limousines, private jets, secluded islands, expansive suites, penthouses, and the best of the glamorous riches that the world has to offer. What you do not expect is that he would look over at a basin, a water pitcher, and a towel. With all that he knew and all that he was, he looked over at a basin, a water pitcher, and a towel.

Do you know that most folks if they had what Jesus had and knew what Jesus knew would not even notice the basin, the water pitcher, and the towel? In some respects in this world, the more you have the less you see. That's why celebrities tint the windows of their limousines as they ride through the neighborhoods of the people that no one is bound to respect. That is why our nation runs roughshod over the poor and downtrodden of the world, offering those without honor a two-dollar tip of what is called "social welfare and entitlements," while spending billions on two wars and fabulous pools of corporate welfare and entitlements, with no end in sight. This is why we can run roughshod over other nations, choosing their leadership and installing democracy at the point of a gun. The more you have the less you see. I am impressed that Jesus looked by the door and even saw the basin, the water pitcher, and the towel as instruments that he would use.

He got up from the meal, took off his outer clothing, and wrapped the towel around his waist. After that, he poured water into a basin and began to wash his disciples' feet. Is this how kings act? Is this how the King of Kings and the Lord of Lords should act? Washing feet was reserved for those of the lowest status and position in the culture; it was reserved for those who had no claim to dignity or honor that anybody was bound to respect. Only those of little value and worth used the basin, the water pitcher, and the towel. This is not how the one who has all dignity and worth acts—the Great I AM with a basin, a water pitcher, and a towel.

His actions call for a moratorium on arrogance in the church. His action suggests that the purpose of power is not status, privilege, and position, but service. He is saying what we do not want to hear, and acting like we do not want to act. He is saying that the greatest expression of love is to serve. When the time came for him to show the full extent of his love—he took the basin, the water pitcher, and the towel.

I think that we have too much arrogance in the church. I think too much of the time of church people is spent worrying about status, privilege, position, and power. I think that many of us come into church and miss the basin, the water pitcher, and the towel that sit at the entrance to the door. If we are not careful, we will think that it is not our task and not our responsibility. We will come to somehow believe that it is beneath us.

I've had more than one member around our church who was too much of a big shot to serve. I had members who were too impressed with themselves to pick up a piece of paper in the parking lot, too impressed with themselves to clean a toilet, too exalted to give up a seat, too self-righteous to embrace a sinner, too proud to say I am sorry, too indignant to forgive, too angry to let it go, too filled with self-importance to do whatever it takes to serve the community, too self-satisfied to involve "those people," too sanctimonious to be inclusive. There is too much pride in the church. There is too much arrogance in the church.

It starts at the pulpit and goes back to the choir, comes down to the musicians' pit, moves to the front rows with the elders and the deacons, it heads on back to main floor, comes on up to the balcony, goes up to the nest where the media folks are, heads on out to the parking lot, heads downstairs to the kitchen, the classrooms, and the youth church. There is so little humility in the church. God says, you want to get into the kingdom? Then you had better learn to pick up the basin, the water pitcher, and the towel. Humility is the only thing that is going to get you into the kingdom. God wants a servant church.

Did you just hear me say servant church? I have heard of every kind of church—black church, megachurch, gigachurch, rural church, suburban church, emerging church, urban church, high church, Anglo church, Pentecostal church, Confessing church, Open and Affirming church, Free church, charismatic church, and more. But I have rarely heard of servant church. Servant church is a remedy to the quest for status, privilege, position, and power that is too much operative in the church and the world. Briefly, I would like to suggest two characteristics of a servant church.

The first characteristic of a servant church is what I call "spotlight theology." The chief characteristic of spotlight theology is that folks at the top in leadership pick up the basin, the water pitcher, and the towel and serve, and servants who normally operate the basin, the water pitcher, and the towel at the bottom can move into leadership positions at the top. There is fluidity as to who is at the top and who is at the bottom. This is the example that Jesus set when he as the leader picked up the basin, the water pitcher, and the towel. He meant that leaders can become servants and servants can become leaders. The ideal is servants who are leaders and leaders who serve.

My wife and I went to the theater. Lighting is very important in theater. There was a particularly poignant scene when, all of a sudden and to our surprise, a person appeared on stage, as if out of nowhere. The person had been there all the time, but until the lighting was directed to the person, this actor was not visible. This meant that somewhere there was a lighting director with a cue sheet who knew when to light various parts of the stage to accomplish the purposes of the plot and narrative. Some characters were in the background and not seen very much and some characters were in the light and in the foreground, depending on the plot of the play.

So it is in the church. God is the great lighting director and will light up certain people in certain scenes to accomplish God's great plan and narrative. God will background some and foreground others. God puts the spotlight on whomever God wants to put the spotlight on to accomplish God's purposes. It might be that we have to go into the background so another leader can come into the foreground. It might be that I might have to decrease so that another can increase. In the servant church, the call of everyone is to serve, and titles and positions are superfluous because God puts us in the spotlight and God will put us in the background. I know that you are good in the spotlight, but how comfortable are you in the background? How well you do when the light is on another person? How good are you at celebrating the victories in someone else's life?

The second characteristic of the servant church is that, when you love something, you pick up the trash yourself. If you see a piece of paper in the parking lot, you do not wait, you do not call somebody and ask to speak to the supervisor in charge of housekeeping—you do it yourself. Would you pick up a piece of paper in the parking lot? Would you clean a toilet? Would you serve in the lowest places in the church or the community? Or is your specialty calling people to insure that someone else is doing the job?

A story is told of Ray Kroc, who started the McDonald's franchises in Chicago. He had the habit of touring and doing surprise inspections to ensure that the McDonald's restaurants would adhere to the strictest standards of cleanliness and professionalism. With no advance warning or notification, he would just show up at a McDonald's. He paid a visit to a McDonald's restaurant on 55th Street, looked out of the window of his tinted black stretch limousine, and saw profuse amounts of paper and trash on the ground. Ray Kroc asked the driver to stop the car, got out of his stretch limousine, picked up the paper, cleaned the parking lot himself, and then got back into his stretch limousine. He was not arrogant; he was not prideful. He could have called somebody; he could have sent somebody; he could have ordered the limo driver to pick up the trash; he could have found the cell number of the franchise owner and called that person; he could have asked the store manager to come out to the car. But no, because he loved McDonald's, he did it himself.

Ray Kroc reminds me of Jesus. The Bible says that the word of God was made flesh, and Jesus cruises our human neighborhood. He does not have tinted windows in his stretch limousine, and he looks out and sees people who because of sin and degradation are considered refuse and trash—people who have no dignity or worth that anybody is bound to respect. Jesus saw you and me out there on the parking lot of life looking and feeling like trash. Jesus could have called somebody. Jesus could have called legions of angels to clean us up. Jesus could have formed a committee. Jesus could have drafted a resolution. But no—he stepped out of that limousine and marched his way to a hill called Calvary and gave his life to clean us up. He did not send somebody; he did not order somebody; he came himself. He took the form of a servant. Philippians 2:6–8 (NIV) says it better:

> [Jesus], being in very nature God, did not consider equality with God something to be grasped, but made himself nothing, taking the very nature of a servant, being made in human likeness. And being found in appearance as a man, he humbled himself by becoming obedient to death—even death on a cross!

When I initially preached this sermon at my former church, after the sermon, a member called me and said that he was convicted by the sermon and was willing to do the lowest job in the church. He said to me that he would be willing to stand in the men's restroom with a towel to serve the needs of people much in the way that at a fine hotel they had attendants. It was the lowest service that he could think of. Then he asked me, "What is the lowest job in the church?" His question puzzled me as I thought about what might be the lowest job in the church. I thought about it. I might need your help; What do you think is the lowest job in the church?

And it dawned on me what to say to him. I said, "The lowest job in the church has already been done." "What is it, pastor?" he asked. "What is the lowest job in the church that has already been done?" "The lowest job in the church," I said, "is the cross at Calvary and it has already been done."

THE BACKSTORY

Modeled after Jesus, the unselfish life of the servant is one of my core beliefs and values about the Christian faith. As a result, I have always gravitated to scriptures, such as this text in John 13:3–5, where the subject is the servant lifestyle. Servanthood and service to others has always been part of my fundamental conviction about the Christian faith.

When I was installed in my first church in 1982, I had the opportunity to choose the scriptural text for the installation service. I was working with an artist to do an original design for the cover for the installation program, and he asked very early for the scriptural text to help stimulate his creativity in design. I shared with him this text that summed up what the installation service meant to me: "For who is greater, the one who is at the table or the one who serves? Is it not the one who is at the table? But I am among you as one who serves" (Luke 22:27). My message was that though I was called to the office of pastor, who had rights as the undershepherd of Christ, my interpretation of that underservice was lowly service itself. I told the church that I was not there to be served, but among them as one who serves.

I took this mandate of lowly service literally, meaning that I placed myself beneath others. What I did not understand until I came into iPEC is that values can either be fear-based or they can be conscious and intentional, or positively based. The challenge was that my humility was based in fear. Humility was for the purpose of seeking approval. The effect of this fear-based humility was that I was not clear about how I want to be treated, not clear about my boundaries, not clear about the vision for my own life, oversensitive to the feelings of others, and overcompensating to avoid conflict. When humility is based in fear, one is not clear about one's inner authority, power, and humility. Fear-based humility is being humble and at the same time asking the questions: Am I good enough? Will they like me? Am I smart enough? One is humble outside in rather than inside out. That kind of humility is looking for outside approval. That kind of humility becomes a "have to" and builds anger, resentment, and even hatred, all the negative feelings that we discussed to in the sermon "Have to vs. Want To."

Let's look deeper at this humility seeking approval. What was it that I was after when I was being humble? My first response would be to please Jesus Christ. I would say that I was following the example of Jesus as mandated by the scriptures. But the covert and the hidden truth was that I really wanted to please people. It is like I was saying to people: like me because I am humble; approve of me because I am willing to serve. Give me applause because I am being just like Jesus. Even though we might express true and spiritual reasons for doing something, it takes a great deal of honesty to admit that the inner or true goal might be something completely based in fear, like the need for approval. T. S. Eliot warns us against this lack of honesty when he says, "The last temptation is the greatest treason. To do the right deed for the wrong reason."[21] I was being humble for the wrong reason.

It was only when I could tell God I was wrong and challenge my belief system about the need for approval that I could make a positive-based decision about my

---

21. T. S. Eliot, *Murder in the Cathedral,* end of act 1.

Christian service. I realized the truth of this statement from the book *Relax, You're Already Perfect:* "To create a new, happier life, all you need is an open mind and the wisdom to challenge the belief system that currently creates your reality."[22]

After challenging my fear-based reality, I discovered that humility could be based in love, and as blasphemous as it sounds, based in the love of self. Humility based in love of self establishes belief in the equality of all. No one is above me and no one is below me. We are all equal. When I choose service out of love rather than fear, it is an intentional choice that allows me to exercise inner authority, be clear about my vision and boundaries, be appropriately sensitive to the feelings of others, and handle conflict as a natural occurrence that can lead to better solutions. I become clear about my own inner authority and power, which means that if you abuse or disregard my offering of service, I can choose not to serve you long before anger and bitterness set it. I can choose not to serve. Despite your disregard, I can still choose to serve, but it will be my choice, and in the fact that I choose, I free myself from the anger, resentment, etc. Service as a choice is a "want to" and not a "have to." Service is a positive action as I serve from love and passion. Service is an intentional choice. This is how Jesus served—as an intentional choice and full of joy.

---

22. Bruce D. Schneider, *Relax, You're Already Perfect: 10 Spiritual Lessons . . . to Remember* (Newburyport, Mass: Hampton Roads Publishing, 2002), 49.

8

RENEW YOUR YES!

The Lord came and stood there, calling as at the other times,
"Samuel, Samuel!" Then Samuel said— "Speak, for your servant
is listening.". . . "What is it he said to you?" Eli asked. "Do not
hide it from me. May God deal with you, be it ever so severely, if
you hide from me anything God told you." So Samuel told him
everything, hiding nothing from him. Then Eli said, "He is the
Lord; let him do what is good in his eyes."

—1 SAMUEL 3:10, 17–18 NIV

The call story of Samuel begins in chapter 1 of 1 Samuel with Elkanah, who had two wives, Hannah and Peninnah. Hannah could not have children, but Peninnah had plenty. Peninnah became Hannah's bitter antagonist and developed the habit of ridiculing Hannah because she could not have children. Hannah, as a result, was completely stressed out. She would weep bitterly and she would not eat. The Bible says that Hannah went to the temple and wept in the bitterness of her soul, saying, "God, if only you would give me a son, then I will make sure that I give him back to you to serve you all the days of his life." Eli, the priest, answered her and said, "Go in peace, and may the God of Israel grant what you have asked." After hearing this from Eli the priest, she went her way and her face was no longer downcast. Husband and wife lay together and Hannah conceived and gave birth to a son—Samuel.

After the boy was weaned, keeping her vow, Hannah gave the boy back to the Lord. And Eli, the same priest who had prophesied over her to have the child, received the child Samuel on behalf of the Lord. Samuel was serving before the Lord, a young boy wearing a linen ephod. He was a young apprentice, a novitiate, a catechist, a minister in training. His mother came to visit him each year when they came up to the temple, and each year she brought him a robe. Eli blessed Hannah, saying, "May the Lord give you more children to replace the one that you gave to the Lord."

The text says that the word of the Lord was rare; there were not many visions, not many revelations from the Lord. Divine revelation was mediated through a seer, prophet, or priest. There were not many revelations from God. And why were there not many revelations? The text implies it was because Eli had two sons who were priests, Hophni and Phineas, and these two sons did evil in the sight of the Lord. It was customary that while a family was boiling the meat from their sacrifice, the priest would come by with a three-prong fork, and whatever the priest would pull from the meat would belong to the priest. Hophni and Phineas told folks they wanted their portion raw before the meat was boiled, and if the people did not agree, they took it by force. They ripped the people off. They also slept with the women who served at the entrance to the tent of meeting. They did evil in God's sight, and the Lord was displeased.

In 1 Samuel 2:27–36, God pronounces a judgment on the house of Eli by sending a prophet to confront Eli because he would not restrain his sons. The prophet said that the Lord would cut short the priesthood of Eli's family. They would be cut off from the altar. There would never be an old man in their family line. His two sons would die on the same day and God would raise up a faithful priest.

In chapter 3, the text comments that the boy Samuel ministered unto the Lord before Eli. The word of the Lord was rare and there were not many visions. Eli's eyes were becoming so weak that he could barely see. Do not miss the implication here: there is no word from the Lord and the priest cannot see. He could not see physically and by implication could not see spiritually. It identifies him as an elderly person of ministry, on the sunset side of his ministry, and almost blind not just from physical age, but from ignoring the sins of his sons. The word of the Lord was rare and the prophet of God could barely see.

Samuel was lying down where the ark of the Lord was. Then the Lord called "Samuel! Samuel!" Samuel said—"Here I am." And he ran to Eli and said, "Here I am. You called me." Eli said, "I did not call you. Go back and lie down." Again the Lord called, "Samuel! Samuel!" Samuel went to Eli again. Eli said, "I did not call you." Now Samuel did not know the Lord because the word of the Lord had not yet been revealed to him. The Lord called Samuel a third time and he again went to Eli. Eli realized that it was the Lord calling, and said to the boy, "Go and lie down and if the Lord calls, then say, 'Speak, Lord, for your servant is listening.'" So Samuel went and lay down in his place. The Lord came and stood there, calling as the other times, "Samuel! Samuel!" Samuel said, "Speak, Lord, for your servant is listening."

Samuel's humility in responding to the call is moving: "Speak Lord, for your servant is listening." Samuel's response exemplifies innocence, purity, brokenness, willingness to serve, and his reverence and the respect for the caller. Speak, Lord; I will go wherever you tell me to go and I will do whatever you tell me to do. Speak, Lord, for thy servant heareth. He did not even know the Lord, but there was such humility and teachable-ness in his spirit. This is the purity of saying "yes" in one's own heart to God. No one can say "yes" for you. You have to say "yes" in your own heart. Speak Lord, for your servant is listening. I do not know what it all means; I am not sure of what it all means, but speak, for I am listening. It reminds me of the text in Isaiah 6 when the Lord asks: "Who shall go for us and whom shall we send?" and the prophet replies, "Here I am, send me."

Do you remember the purity of your call? Do you remember when you first said "yes"? Do you remember when it did not matter how much money you made or what, if any, the pay level was, you just wanted to please God? You wanted to do what God wanted you to do. I do—I remember the excitement and the fear and the trembling. Speak, Lord, for your servant is listening. I was once Samuel.

However, this call text is not just about Samuel; it is also about Eli. When God speaks with Samuel, God tells Samuel that God will carry out the prophecy in chapter 2 against Eli and his two sons, Hophni and Phineas. God told Samuel of the judgment upon Eli's ministry because he did nothing to restrain his children. This is what seasoned servants of the Gospel experience—judgment on their ministry. After the season of the purity of the call, there comes in the middle to the closing years of ministry the judgment of the call. God shows us where we are wrong. And sometimes we look more like Eli than we do Samuel. In the eyes of God, Eli was wrong.

Now, Eli was not a bad priest. We see him in action blessing Hannah in chapter 1. In response to her weeping for a child, he says, "Be blessed and may it be done to as you prayed." Hannah goes home and conceives a son. Eli was not a bad priest. Hannah comes back and brings the boy to serve. Eli accepts the boy and blesses the family. Eli was not a bad priest. Then the momma brings the boy a robe each year and Eli blesses her and says, "You will have more children because you gave Samuel to the Lord." He is not a bad priest. He is walking with this family, providing pastoral care and nurture to this family. He is mentoring Samuel. He is a good priest.

He is a good priest, but not a good parent. He will not discipline his sons. All of us have shortcomings; all of us make mistakes; all of us have places where were we struggle to meet the standard. Some of us have been so busy caring for the church, the business, or our professional life that we neglected our families and some of our children have become Hophni and Phineas. Some of us have saved other people's children, but could not save our own. Some of us have allowed church leaders to act like Hophni and Phineas and we did nothing and said nothing. Can I be real about it—some of us here have gotten too close to the women or the men who are serving at the temple and some things have happened that had no business happening. Some of us have become distracted and our enthusiasm and zeal for ministry have waned. Some of us have lost our sense of authority and have stifled our own gifts.

We are good priests. We do a whole lot of good things for people. We minister the Word, share the sacraments, commit ashen bodies back unto the Lord, bless babies, and consummate weddings. We walk hospital floors, sometimes in the wee hours of the morning, pray when the diagnosis is cancer, pass handkerchiefs and Kleenex when the tears are flowing fast and furious, bring hope to the hopeless, and are a friend to the friendless. We rail against injustices against the poor, declare righteousness where there is oppression, decry sin and disobedience to God, and sit in courtrooms with members who have made mistakes. Despite all of this, we know that there are places where our ministry has not measured up. We know faults, flaws, mistakes, and shortcomings.

There is more that we could have accomplished. There was more that we could have done. Either we were too soft as a leader, or we were too hard. Either we quit too early, or we stayed too long. Either we were too dictatorial, or we were not assertive enough. This is the anguish of those of us who are seasoned. This is the anguish of Eli. And sometimes, we, like Eli, wonder if there are any visions from the Lord. Sometimes we believe that a Word from the Lord is rare. I was once Samuel, but I feel more like Eli. I was once Samuel, but I believe myself to be Eli.

In verse 17, Samuel lay down until morning. He was afraid to tell Eli the vision. But Eli called him and said, "Samuel, my son, what did the Lord say to you? Do not hide it from me. Tell me everything." So Samuel told him everything. Hiding nothing, he told him that God was judging his family. He uttered the fulfillment of the prophecy that Eli had already heard.

It is amazing to me what Eli said in response to the news about judgment, "He is the Lord, let him do what is good in his eyes." In short, Eli affirmed that the Lord's judgments are right. Let the Lord do what the Lord wants to do. In essence he is saying the same thing Samuel said, "Speak Lord, for your servant is listening." How tough and heart-wrenching that in the face of judgment of his entire ministry, Eli says, "Speak, Lord, for your servant is listening." Here again we see the purity of the call, the innocence, the humility, and the reverence and respect for the caller. After all those years of ministry, after all of the mistakes, and coming face to face with his shortcomings, he says, "Speak, Lord, for thy servant heareth." That is how I started out when the Lord called me and that is how I will end it when God has passed the ministry on to a younger person, "Speak, Lord, thy servant heareth." Despite my shortcomings, I will say, "Speak, Lord, for your servant is listening." Eli renewed his "yes." In effect, he is saying, "My soul says yes."

The good news is the call. The good news is that we do not make the call, the call makes us. The good news is that it is not about us, it is about the call. The good news is that, despite our mistakes and our shortcomings, it is it still about the call. The revelation of the Lord must come to the people, so the Lord calls. The Lord fashions seers, prophets, and priests through whom the word of the Lord will come. It is not that we are that smart, or strong, or educated, or deep; it is that the Lord needs somebody. It is not that we are perfect or we have it all together, but the Lord needs somebody.

The prophet Isaiah in 40:6–8 says, "All of us are like grass. The grass withers and the flowers fade, but the word of our God stands forever."

Paul, in the second letter to the Corinthians, in 4:7, says, "But we have this treasure in jars of clay to show that this all-surpassing power is from God and not from us." And in 2 Corinthians 12:9, "But he said to me, 'My grace is sufficient for you, for my power is made perfect in weakness.' Therefore I will boast all the more gladly about my weaknesses, so that Christ's power may rest on me."

We do not make the call, but the call makes us. If you are a Samuel, all you can do is say "yes." If you are an Eli, you can only renew your "yes."

Yes, to your will; yes to your way.

Yes, if you call me to serve ten thousand.

Yes, if you call me to serve a hundred.

Yes, if I am successful; yes, if I fail.

Yes, if I am right; yes, if I am wrong.

Yes if I am up; yes, if I am down.

Yes, if I am young; yes, if I am old.

Yes, in my darkness; yes, in my despair.

Yes, in my laughter; yes, in my tears.

Yes, if I am Samuel; yes, if I am Eli.

Yes, Lord, yes—my soul says yes.

THE BACKSTORY

There is one sentence in this sermon that resonates deeply in my heart: "I was once Samuel, and now I am Eli." This statement is an indication of my feeling that I am a mid- to late-career pastor who is seeking to come face to face with shortcomings, mistakes, flaws, and blindness in my person and ministry. For me, the fault was the fear of my own authority. Like Eli, who would not discipline his own sons, I would not discipline my own fear, which was running rampant in my inner life.

In a coaching session, I talked about the pain and guilt around the fact that I had not trusted in my own inner authority. The coach asked me if there was another way to interpret my perception of my lack of inner authority. The coach reminded me of our work around NAE (neutral activating events—see the backstory of "Have to vs. Want To") and suggested that there are many ways to interpret any event and my interpretation of events had to do with my consciousness. I was at a loss for an alternate interpretation and asked for any suggestions.

The coach said that I had lasted eighteen years at my former church and thirteen at my present church and that totaled thirty-one years of pastoral leadership. It seemed to the coach that I could not last in leadership for this length of time if I did not have the ability, in some measure, to exercise my own authority. It would seem, by my longevity in ministry, that if I believed in something, then I am strong enough and have enough inner authority to get it done. What if it were true that if I did not exert my authority, it meant that I did not really believe in what I was trying to accomplish?

The coach wondered if my lack of authority was an indication to myself that there was not alignment between who I am at my core and what I am doing (backstory of "Have to vs. Want To"). What if what I was doing did not match up with what I know to be true and what I wanted, really? Could it be that waffling was connected to not being sure of my passion? Waffling indicates the need for an assessment of what I believe to be true. What do I want, really? What do I want to do with my life? Where am I headed? What is it that I value? Waffling is not a quality that I have to fix; it is an indication from my inner life that something is not matching up with who I am. It might be that I am vague and unclear as to what I really believe. Being unclear about what I really believe leads to not being clear about boundaries and my own inner authority, making myself lower than others, desiring approval from others, and seeking avoidance of conflict. Might it be that somewhere in my life, I am experiencing misalignment of values, that is, misalignment of who I am with what I am trying to accomplish?

I gave deep thought to what it would take to stop waffling, get clear, make decisions, and exercise inner authority. I diagrammed my reflections and entitled the new style of leadership as "passionate engagement." Passionate engagement is the alignment of who I am and what I do that we discussed in "Have to vs. Want To," in the last section. Passionate engagement is energetic engagement at the highest level (see Figure 4).

FIGURE 4: BUILDING MY LIFE FROM THE INSIDE OUT: PASSIONATE ENGAGEMENT

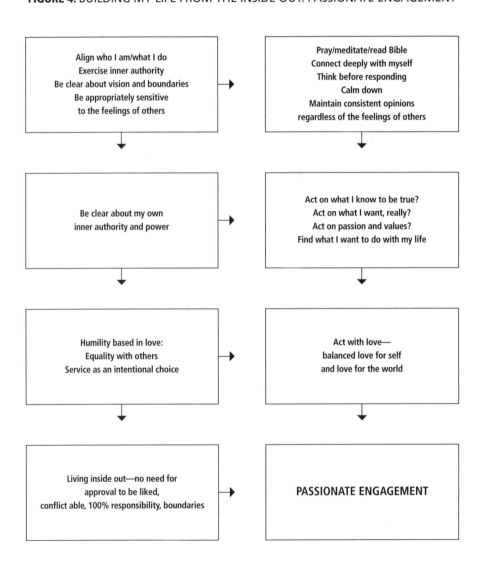

I decided to settle the question of alignment: what I was doing did not align with my values. I was no longer going to be a senior pastor. I decided to exercise my inner authority, be clear about my vision and boundaries, and be appropriately sensitive to the feelings of others. I determined to do what I know to be true and what I want, really. I decided that humility and service would be an intentional choice based in love rather than fear. I would balance love for myself and love for the world, which I have come to call self-care. I made the choice to live inside out with less need to be liked, less need to seek approval from others, and less avoiding of conflict. I resolved that I am 100 percent "response-able." I would lead a life of passionate engagement. The opposite of waffling in leadership is passionate engagement. I would align who I am in my inner core with what I am doing in the world. I would "renew my yes" by leaving the ministry of pastoring a congregation.

part three

EXECUTING THE CHOICE

◆ 9 ◆

THE SPIRITUAL ONES

Live creatively, friends. If someone falls into sin, forgivingly restore him/her, saving your critical comments for yourself. You might be needing forgiveness before the day is out. Stoop down and reach out to those who are oppressed. Share their burdens, and so complete Christ's law. If you think you are too good for that, you are badly deceived. Make a careful exploration of who you are and the work you have been given, and then sink yourself into that. Do not be impressed with yourself. Don't compare yourself with others. Each of you must take responsibility for doing the creative best you can with your own life.

—GALATIANS 6:1–5 MSG

Beginning in the first verse of the fifth chapter of Galatians, Paul exhorts the Galatians to live the life of freedom for which Christ has set them free. Paul worries that in attempting to fulfill the law, with practices such as circumcision, Christians were squandering the gift of Christ's freedom. Living by our own religious plans and projects cuts us off from freedom in Christ. That freedom does not mean that we can do any act or practice, because such license destroys our freedom. The purpose of our freedom in Christ is to serve one another and the world in love.

If the Galatians would live freely, motivated by God's Spirit, they would not feed the compulsions of the flesh based in selfishness. The freedom of Christ and our own selfishness cannot exist in the same person. We will either serve one or the other. Paul encourages the Galatians to choose freedom in Christ and give up a law-dominated selfish existence. In verse 19 of Galatians 5, Paul lists the characteristics of a selfish existence, what is traditionally known as the "works of the flesh": sexual immorality, impurity, debauchery, idolatry, witchcraft, hatred, discord, jealousy, fits of rage, selfish ambition, dissentions, factions, envy, drunkenness, orgies, and the like. Paul says, "I warn you as I did before that those who live like this will not inherit the kingdom of God."

Galatians 5:19–21, in Eugene Peterson's paraphrase, *The Message*, defines the works of the flesh as "the selfish existence" trying to get its way all the time. Peterson identifies the characteristics of the selfish existence thus:

It is obvious what kind of life develops out of trying to get your own way all the time: repetitive, loveless, cheap sex; a stinking accumulation of mental and emotional garbage; frenzied and joyless grabs for happiness; trinket gods; magic-show religion; paranoid loneliness; cutthroat competition; all-consuming-yet-never-satisfied wants; a brutal temper; an impotence to love or be loved; divided homes and divided lives; small-minded and lopsided pursuits; the vicious habit of depersonalizing everyone into a rival; uncontrolled and uncontrollable addictions; ugly parodies of community. I could go on.

In verse 22, Paul acknowledges the characteristics of those who live in the freedom of Christ, traditionally what we call the "fruit of the Spirit": love, joy, peace, forbearance, kindness, goodness, faithfulness, gentleness and self-control. Paul admonishes the Galatians not to be selfish, becoming conceited, provoking and envying each other, but to lead Spirit-filled lives of freedom in Christ characterized by the fruit of the Spirit.

The Message translates the fruit of the Spirit, or freedom in Christ, as "to live God's way" and gives characteristics of that life in Galatians 5:22–23:

But what happens when we live God's way? He brings gifts into our lives, much the same way that fruit appears in an orchard—things like affection for others, exuberance about life, serenity. We develop a willingness to stick with things, a sense of compassion in the heart, and a conviction that a basic holiness permeates things and people. We find ourselves involved in loyal commitments, not needing to force our way in life, able to marshal and direct our energies wisely.

Since the Galatians, by virtue of their confession of faith, have chosen freedom in Christ, Paul tells them to make sure that freedom is not just an idea in their heads or a sentimental emotion in their hearts. He challenges them to work out this freedom in every detail of their lives. In closing chapter 5, he warns them not to compare themselves to others, because each and every Christian is an original.

We walk now into the first verse of the sixth chapter, the focal verses for the sermon. Peterson starts the first verse with the admonition "Live creatively, friends." To live life out of the freedom in Christ takes a great deal of creativity. To live our lives as an original and walk in our freedom in Christ takes tremendous creativity. Paul constructs a hypothetical scenario to demonstrate the kind of creativity that it takes to walk in the freedom of Christ. He asks: What would you do if you found a brother or a sister caught in a flaw, fault, or sin? One option is to overlook the situation and pretend that it's not happening. The result of this option is that the sin continues unabated and lives are destroyed. The other option is to publicly expose the sin to the community. This option runs the risk of the appearance of superior righteousness. When one openly exposes other people's sin, one can easily look morally superior. Paul suggests that for the creative person, the one who walks in the freedom of Christ, there is a third imaginative option: to restore the person gently. Paul calls the ones who have the imaginative and resourceful ability to restore people gently the *spiritual ones,* or the mature ones. Paul suggests that if you consider yourself to be a spiritual one, specifically, if you consider yourself to be in a place of spiritual leadership and maturity, you must creatively restore people gently. This is how you test your spiritual maturity: Do you have the freedom, creativity, and imaginative capacity to restore someone gently?

The Greek word for "restore" is the same word that is used for a broken bone that is set in place to be healed. Paul says when people are caught in a flaw or a sin, they are broken off from the body much like a broken bone. It is the job of the spiritual ones to put an imaginative cast around a broken person, to surround a person with an inventive healing spirit of forgiveness and gentleness that allows the person to reconnect back with the body.

The ones who are spiritual creatively restore people according to freedom in Christ. The spiritual ones do not gossip about people, or make fun of people by spreading their faults and flaws. Paul suggests that we restore people gently because, as my grandmother said, "folks who live in glass houses should not throw stones." In other words, resourcefully restore people and watch yourself, lest you be tempted. No one is beyond temptation. No one is beyond falling or making mistakes. Paul advocates an attitude of humility, creativity, forgiveness, and love when we encounter flaws, faults, and sin in other people's lives, because all of us live by the mercy and grace of God. This is how you know that you are spiritual: you express the freedom and creativity of Christ to restore people in love and gentleness.

Another expression of the freedom and creativity of the spiritual ones is found in verse 2: bear one another's burdens. Spiritual people bear the burdens of others. Spiritual people creatively share the load with someone whenever temptation is wearing a person out. Life will wear all of us out and tear us down to the point that we will yield to temptation if someone does not help us carry the burden. For example, I was invited as a guest speaker to a marvelous church pastored by a fabulous preacher and pastor. As he drove me to the airport, he requested a conversation with me later that night. He called and confessed that he was preparing to go outside of his marriage. They had already both agreed and had set the date, time, and place, but when the word of God was preached that morning, he was convicted that it was wrong, and he decided to talk to me. I told him gently, with compassionate tears running down my face, that I understood how he could feel this way, but sin is never the answer and never worth the momentary pleasure. I didn't quote scripture to judge and condemn him. I cried with him and told him yielding to temptation is a dead end street. I had prayer with him. I followed up with him and prayed with him three times a week over a protracted period of time until he came through the trial. I creatively bore his burden. I shared the load with him. I never called his name or situation to anybody. I carried the burden of his temptation between just him and me.

If freedom in Christ and creativity in living is what Paul defines as a spiritual person, what keeps us from becoming spiritual persons? In verses 3 and 4, Paul argues that conceit keeps us from fulfilling our role as spiritual ones. We think more highly of ourselves than we ought to think. We think that the important aspect of leadership is to exercise power and authority and almost completely ignore that we must carry the infirmity of the weak. Often, we have become so caught up in the status and privilege of our leadership position that we forget how easily temptation can besiege and beset us all. We look down on people who struggle because we ignore our temptations and justify to ourselves that based upon our exalted leadership position we are beyond the temptations and struggles of common people. We think more highly of ourselves than we ought to think. We are impressed with ourselves.

The second thing that keeps us from freedom in Christ and creativity in living is comparing ourselves and our work to other people. Paul starts this discussion in the last verses of chapter 5: ". . . we will not compare ourselves with each other as if one of us were better and another worse. We have far more interesting things to do with our lives. Each of us is an original." It's harmful to the spiritual life when you compare yourself to other people. On one side, you are going to find somebody who looks worse off than you, and you are going to feel superior and think you are better. On the other side, you will find someone who is better off than you, and you will experience low self-esteem, inferiority, and intimidation. The bottom line is that when you compare yourself to someone else, you judge yourself in comparison to him/her. One person said it this way: "Every time we compare ourselves with someone, we can never measure up because we're comparing our insides with their outsides." I look at myself on the inside and see the fear, uncertainty, and struggle that I am living with. But, then, when I look at another person on the outside, he/she looks happy and contented, and seems to be enjoying life. But I really do not have any idea what's going on inside of the other person. Most of us compare how inadequate we feel on the inside with how others look like they have it all together on the outside. Let me say it plain: you're judging! You're judging yourself and you're judging the other person, and you will never develop your freedom and creativity in Christ as long as you're judging in this manner.

The most dangerous part of judging ourselves and other people is the result that we compete with each other. When we compete with each other, we demonstrate the characteristics of the works of the flesh and a selfish existence expressed in Galatians 5:19: sexual immorality, impurity, debauchery, idolatry, witchcraft, hatred, discord, jealousy, fits of rage, selfish ambition, dissentions, factions, envy, drunkenness, orgies, and the like. Remember, Paul said those who live like this will not inherit the kingdom of God. God never intended for us to compete with one another. God intended freedom in Christ expressing itself in creativity and love.

From the inside out, every believer is an original and therefore implements Christ's freedom in his/her life in a different way. Every believer as part of freedom in Christ has a task from the Lord and is responsible to the Lord for the living out of this task. The spiritual ones exercise their freedom in Christ with imagination from the inside out. They follow the admonition of Paul:

> Make a careful exploration of who you are and the work you have been given, and then sink yourself into that. Don't be impressed with yourself. Don't compare yourself with others. Each of you must take responsibility for doing the creative best you can with your own life.

Each of us has an original and unique task, a calling from the Lord. We have the responsibility to the Lord to creatively do what we have been called to do. We have the freedom in Christ to make a careful exploration of who we are and the work that we have been given. The spiritual ones are people who live in the freedom and creativity for which Christ has set them free, and then sink themselves into the work that they have been given. They have far more interesting things to do with their lives than being impressed with themselves, or comparing their lives with others. They take responsibility for doing the creative best that they can with their own lives.

Based upon our freedom in Christ, you and I are on a creative journey. Our lives cannot look like the lives of others. God has a unique call on us, a specific role for us, something special just for us. There's a reason you like to cook, read, teach, sew, serve, preach, paint, go out to the mission field, etc. It's part of your unique calling. It is part of the uniqueness that makes you who you are. I am calling you to walk in your freedom in Christ. As long as you've got your eyes on everybody else, you're distracting yourself from your uniqueness. You are distracting your life with outside in perspectives rather than living inside out. I am calling you to live creatively, friends. You are one of the spiritual ones. I admonish you in the words of *The Message*:

> Live creatively, friends. If someone falls into sin, forgivingly restore him/her, saving your critical comments for yourself. You might be needing forgiveness before the day is out. Stoop down and reach out to those who are oppressed. Share their burdens and so complete Christ's law. If you think you are too good for that, you are badly deceived. Make a careful exploration of who you are and the work you have been given and then sink yourself into that. Do not be impressed with yourself. Don't compare yourself with others. Each of you must take responsibility for doing the creative best you can with your own life.

THE BACKSTORY

Once a pastor walks in freedom and imaginatively makes the decision to transition, one of the most critical questions that emerge for both pastor and congregation is: how can the pastor leave well? When I say leave well, I point to primarily three specific areas of concern from the perspective of the pastor.

First is obtaining relationship closure with both those who supported and loved the pastor and those who did not. Every church has people in both camps. Some members are very sad to see the pastor leave, and others believe the church will do better under new leadership.

Second, it is important for the pastor to take an objective assessment of the personal strengths and challenges of the pastor and the pastor's ministry in the ministry context. By this process, the pastor learns critical lessons for the next place of ministry and the maturing of the pastor's own life and soul.

Lastly, the pastor advocates for positive and constructive transition to help the congregation and the new pastor have the best chance at a successful relationship and ministry.

One of the most creative measures for me was the insight that leaving well could be helped by an objective outside person functioning as consultant to both the church and the pastor. The congregation and the pastor were going through the myriad of emotions of transition, and it was very difficult to be objective. As a result, the services of Dr. Carl George functioned to assist Mississippi Boulevard Christian Church and myself with this pastoral transition.

Initially, Carl George was hired as a consultant to help us grapple with a decline in worship attendance at our main campus. Our east campus was growing phenomenally and we wanted someone to take a fresh look at what could be done to help both of our campuses have outstanding growth. In the midst of the growth conversation, I informed Carl George that I believed God was leading me to retire from pastoral ministry. He immediately began to work with me on how I might transition well. What I could not recognize was how much creativity and interior work would need to be done above and beyond the work that I had done that I have talked about in the first two sections of this book to make the necessary decisions to leave well.

In July 2009, three years before my announcement to retire and leave the church on July 2, 2012, I informed key leaders that I did not feel I had energy beyond three more years of service as senior pastor. I assured them that I knew the levels of energy that it took to fulfill the role of senior pastor and ensure a growing and thriving ministry. I was honest with them and told them that I only had three more years of energy. Based upon our conversation, we agreed that on June 30, 2012, I was to inform the church leadership as to whether I would retire or continue to serve as senior pastor. The contractual agreement that I had with the church would expire on December 31, 2012, and six months before that date, it would be helpful to the leadership to know my decision and intent.

In December 2010, two full years before December 31, 2012, I began preparing the leadership for my transition. I sent key leaders the book *The Elephant in* the Boardroom: Speaking the Unspoken about Pastoral Transition.[23] The critical point of the book is that the elephant in the church boardroom was not *if* the pastor was going to leave, but *when* the pastor was going to leave. The book helps pastors and leaders to develop a wise and constructive plan for this eventuality. This book was helpful in all of our thinking as we all marched to the June 30, 2012, decision date.

In March 2012, key leaders and I started informal meetings to talk about what I might say on June 30, 2012. I told them that in all likelihood, on June 30, 2012, I would tell them that I was going to retire. With that information, we decided to put together a transition plan that could be implemented upon my announcement, if indeed retirement was my decision. It took us until June 1, 2012 to finalize the transition plan. This left all in readiness, except my prayer, searching for God's will, input from my family, and my final decision.

On June 30, I delivered a letter to the church moderator informing her of my decision to retire as of December 31, 2012. Meetings were held immediately the next evening with the church council and the elders and subsequently on July 2 with the congregation to inform them of my decision. The transition plan was implemented, and this left us six months to negotiate leaving well.

Initially, six months seemed like a long time. The standard advice given to pastors is to stay no more than sixty to ninety days after the announcement, because "lame duck" status is very painful. In Free Church institutions, churches without hierarchy of bishops and the like, the pastor very discreetly secures a new position, informs the church, and gives a minimal amount of time for transition. Many of these transitions become emotional, and decisions are made under duress because one of the most difficult aspects of congregational life is the transition of a senior pastor, for which there usually has been very little planning.

I thought that we could do it creatively and differently, and the "lame duck" status could be an imaginative and positive experience, as it gave time for a thoughtful and careful leaving, which would be of great benefit to me, my family, the congregation, and the next pastor. Because we had six months, we made the thoughtful decision, for example, to hire an executive search firm to streamline the search process. Usually the search process for a new pastor takes about eighteen

---

23. Carol Weese and J. Russell Crabtree, *The Elephant in the Boardroom: Speaking the Unspoken about Pastoral Transition* (Hoboken, NJ: John Wiley & Sons, 2004).

to twenty-four months, but we believed that we could shorten the process and drastically improve the candidate pool if we approached the search with professional help. From the time of my announcement to leave, July 2, 2012, to the announcement of the new pastor, January 14, 2013, it took seven months. This short time frame is almost unheard of, but careful planning allows for the best decision.

Six months gave adequate time for the church and me to say goodbye. We could work through the stages of the grieving process. I had no idea of the emotional hurdles even in a healthy separation that I would encounter. It was hard and emotional to let go of my decision-making authority and, in essence, become a consultant to plans and program beyond my tenure. It was difficult to go through a series of lasts—this was the last time I was going to do this or the last time I was going to do that. It was tough to watch people whose lives were intricately bound up with mine and realize that, in a few months, I would see them much less often. I did not know that Carl George as a sounding board and coach was going to be so instrumental in my leaving well. I did not know that I could rise to the level of a "spiritual one" and become so creative in addressing the reality of my retirement. I did not know that I would not have many possibilities to compare myself to others because the way that we were approaching the transition was so very creative, and imaginative decisions had to be made on a regular basis. I could not think more highly of myself, and I would have to do the creative best that I could to transition well because there was no roadmap to our approach. I had to make a careful exploration of my life and the work that I was given to do (transition) and take responsibility to live creatively.

In the next several backstories, I will talk more about relationship closure with both those who supported and loved the pastor and those who did not, an appropriate assessment of the personal strengths and challenges of the pastor's ministry in the ending ministry context, and positive and constructive approaches to transitions to help the congregation and the new pastor have the best chance at a successful relationship. The sum total of it all was that I wanted to walk in the freedom for which Christ had set me free and take responsibility for doing the creative best I could with my own life.

✦ I O ✦

THE SPIRITUAL LIFE

Make a careful exploration of who you are and the work you

have been given, and then sink yourself into that.... Each of you

must take responsibility for doing the creative best you can with

your own life.   —GALATIANS 6:4–5 MSG

The spiritual life is inside out and not outside in. To live inside out is to ask two fundamental questions. The first is: what do you know at the core of your being to be true? Many people profess from their lips one truth and when you watch how they actually behave you see another truth. I am more interested in how you live than in what you say.

Let me give you an example of what I mean when I ask what you know to be true. The doctor has called you back after the second mammogram to give you the results of the biopsy of the lump in your breast. The doctor tells you the test results confirm that you have cancer. You have to tell yourself something to get up and walk out of the doctor's office. Based upon the news, what you want to do is fall apart. What you want to do is go ahead and die right at that very moment. However, you have to tell yourself something. You go down on the inside, to your very gut and core, and tell yourself something. What you tell yourself is what you know to be true. It is only what you know to be true at the very core

94

of your being that will give you the courage to walk out of that office, fight cancer, and go on living. One woman told me that what she knew to be true was that God was a healer, and that was the only truth that gave her the courage to walk out of the doctor's office. What is it that you know at the core of your being to be true? The spiritual life begins at the point that you answer this question.

The second question you must answer to live inside out is: what do I want, really? Notice the word "really." I know what you want. You want what we all want, what our flesh wants in its selfish existence. Our selfish existence wants to overvalue immediate gains (like a new pair of shoes) at the cost of future expenses (high interest rates). Our selfish existence is thrilled by the prospect of immediate reward and therefore wants to max out the credit card, order dessert, and smoke a cigarette. The selfish existence tells people to take out a mortgage they cannot afford, buy a car to impress people, or run up debt when they should be saving for retirement. The selfish existence wants a reward, and wants it now, regardless of the long-term consequences. Your selfish existence does not want to get up off that couch, get up out of that bed, and get on that treadmill or exercise to improve your health and overall wellness. The selfish existence doesn't want to fast and pray. It does not want any part of fasting and praying because the body has to do without while you fast and pray. Your selfish existence wants to gratify its selfish desires. This is what your selfish existence wants. So, it's not what you want. It's what you want, really.

What I want, really, is to live God's way. Following *The Message* in Galatians 5:22–23, I want the gifts of God in my life the way that fruit appears in an orchard. What I want, really, is a sense of compassion in the heart, a conviction that a basic holiness permeates things and people. I want to be involved in loyal commitments and not need to force my way in life. I want the promise of God that I can have exuberance about life, serenity, and a willingness to stick with things. This is what I want, really.

If these characteristics of freedom in Christ are available, why are we leading such dull, uncreative lives? I believe that most people are content to live their lives by a template from the outside imposed by other people. Many people live according to what they see other people do. Many people live according to what the advertisers and marketers tell us is the essence of happiness, joy, and a meaningful life. Somebody told us that if we put a designer label or designer brand clothing on our bodies, then we are somebody. So we spend our lives trying to prove to other people that we are somebody based upon the material things that we can accumulate and own. We medicate our lives with stuff and things. If we are not careful, we will live dull and uncreative lives based on a template that is outside in and not inside out.

I believe that, living inside out in the freedom of Christ, I can be creative with my own life and not need to uncritically accept a template from other people. Our text for this sermon, Galatians 6:4–5, reinforces this belief when it says:

> Make a careful exploration of who you are and the work you have been given and then sink yourself into that. . . . Each of you must take responsibility for doing the creative best you can with your own life.

I accept the responsibility to do the creative best with my life. This means that if I am miserable, the responsibility falls on me to live creatively. If I am unhappy, sad, or depressed, then that has nothing to do with anyone else. It is not anyone else's fault that my life is dull and uncreative. It is my responsibility to live creatively, to live inside out.

We have been using the word creative, but what does the word "creative" mean? It means relating to or involving the imagination or original ideas. It means being inventive or productive of something fresh and unusual. Being creative is seeing the same thing as everybody else, but thinking something different. Didn't Apple have that as a motto—"Think different"? Look at how, by thinking differently, they have made products that have changed the world. Listen to this: *to be creative is to be inspired and see in your mind something that does not exist and act with determination, faith, energy, and passion to bring it into existence.*

In the context of the spiritual life, being creative means to use your gifts given by the Creator to express yourself from the inside out and not let the world label you from the outside in. How creative have you been about your life? How imaginative have you been about your life? How fresh is your life? I know how fresh your clothes are, but how fresh is your life? I know how fresh your apartment/condo/home is, but how fresh is your life? Are you leading an original and creative life? Are you using your gifts given to you by the Creator to express yourself from the inside out and not allowing the world to label you from the outside in? In your spiritual life, be creative with your own life from the inside out.

In the last sermon, "The Spiritual Ones," I identified in Galatians 5:25 that Eugene Peterson has Paul tell the Galatians to make sure that freedom in Christ is not just an idea in their heads or a sentimental emotion in their hearts. Paul challenges them to work out this freedom in every detail of their lives. I want to practically demonstrate how freedom in Christ and being creative with your own life from inside out can be worked out in the details of the reader's life. There are four areas in which you must take responsibility and live out your free and creative spiritual life.

First, you must be creative in your *finances*. One of the most important aspects of financial creativity is to realize that debt is bondage. While the rich have the ability to be "independently wealthy," true independence for the middle class and the poor is the ability to live without debt. I realize that debt is necessary at certain critical junctures in life. I realize that there is good debt, such as mortgages, school loans, business loans, and so on, and there is bad debt such as credit cards, payday loans, etc. I realize that debt allows us to innovate, create new products, and, when successful, create new jobs. I advocate and support the responsible use of debt. But after the Great Recession, I watched how banks were bailed out by taxpayers based on being "too big to fail," and then those same banks foreclosed on the homes of American citizens who loaned them the money in the first place. I saw how the "sins" of Wall Street and banks were "forgiven" by a generous government and beneficent taxpayers, but the "sins" of average people were and still are being counted against them in foreclosures, court judgments, and ruined credit reports. I determined that the only freedom I can have is to owe no one. I resolved in my heart to get out of debt as fast as I could. I would suggest the principle of 10-10-80. Give 10 percent of your income to God (tithe), keep 10 percent to invest, pay cash, build your net worth, and live off of 80 percent of what you make. I am an apostle of debt-free living.

Second, you have to be creative with your *physical health and wellness*, including diet, exercise, and a program of preventive maintenance. There is a hospital room waiting for all of us. There is some surgical procedure that has our name on it. Why? Because the body breaks down across time and no one has beaten old age; sooner or later, most of us will be hooked up to machines and IV's, with nurses coming in and out in the middle of the night. The only thing that you can control is what shape you are in when you get to the hospital. The better physical shape you are in, the better chance that you have for recovery. To live inside out, you must be creative with your physical wellness, eat healthier foods, maintain an exercise regimen, and make sure you get regular checkups for preventive, and if necessary, corrective maintenance. We must situate our freedom in Christ in our physical bodies and health.

Next, we must be creative in our *vocation and careers*. Far too many of us live in something called vocational despair. Vocational despair is when we are on the job for the money or because we cannot quit based upon the responsibility that we have. This is living, what we called earlier, "have to" rather than "want to." We do not like the job or career, but we are doing it. For many of us there is a time when we do what we have to do so that we can get to do what we want to do. The faster you know what you want to do, the faster you can get the preparation in place (training, school, etc.), and be ready for the time when you can do what you want to do.

Frederick Buechner asserts that vocation is the place where your deep gladness meets the world's deep hunger.[24] To live creatively and live inside out is to adopt as your vocation the place where your deep gladness meets a deep need in the world. There's a difference between vocation and a job. Vocation is where the deep gladness in you meets the deep despair in the world.

Finally, we must be creative in our *spiritual lives*. Recently, I spent an entire day in hospitals visiting people. I saw that most of the illness and the sickness people were dealing with was unplanned. Cancer is not planned. It's an unexpected interruption in life, and when it unexpect-

---

24. Parker J. Palmer, *Let Your Life Speak: Listening for the Voice of Vocation* (San Francisco: Jossey-Bass, 2000), 16.

edly interrupts your life, you've got to be creative. You have to be creative and work cancer into your life journey. A divorce most of the time is unplanned. The death of a spouse most of the time is unplanned. Your spiritual life has to bring creative resources to bear on the unexpected and the unplanned in life.

Joan Chittister explains that there are some people who accept reality so that the spiritual life can happen in them.[25] She suggests that the spiritual life can only happen when you accept reality. When we accept reality, with creativity we can make an unplanned interruption into meaningful living and growth. Chittister says when we live creatively, at some point we can say, for example, that this cancer is more grace than I can bear. What I do not know is that this pain and tragedy is one of the greatest gifts to me. I just don't know it yet! It's this loss that will open up a whole new world in me. This loss opens up new levels of spiritual life that I would not have had access to. It opens up new levels of creativity and trust in God. The spiritual life is about accepting reality and becoming somebody new to deal with it. This is the spiritual life: freedom and creativity in Christ to harness every experience in life, even tragedy and pain, to our benefit and good.

I believe that creativity in your finances, physical self, vocation, and spiritual life is how freedom in Christ from inside out can be worked out in the details of the reader's life. This is the spiritual life. Galatians 6:4–5 invites us to freedom in Christ:

> Make a careful exploration of who you are and the work you have been given, and then sink yourself into that. Don't be impressed with yourself. Don't compare yourself with others. Each of you must take responsibility for doing the creative best you can with your own life.

THE BACKSTORY

In the last backstory, I suggested that there were three aspects to pastoral transition and leaving well. In this backstory, I want to focus on relationship closure

---

25. Chittister, *Scarred by Struggle*, 57–60.

with both those who support and love the pastor and those who find the pastor's ministry distasteful and are excited to see the pastor leave. Usually, when we talk about relationship closure, we talk about forgiving enemies, establishing boundaries after leaving, managing congregational anxiety, planning healing celebrations, etc., all the while using the metaphor of grief as the backdrop. Robert Creech, in "Bowen Theory and Pastoral Transition," rejects the metaphor of grief to describe pastoral transition.[26] He rejects the metaphor of grief because his leaving was not death and he would have occasion to connect with the congregation again. Instead, he suggests that gratitude is an alternative perspective to grief as the main paradigm through which we could look at leaving and departing. The word that best illustrates my departure from the church is "choice." I will couple the word "choice" with "gratitude" and suggest this creative synergy as a paradigm for relationship closure with a congregation.

Ultimately, all coaching is about the discovery and implementation of choice. People get mired down in the anxious details of their own lives and forget that they have a choice. The coach helps them to remember, create, and access available choices, as well as foster the accountability that helps them to implement their choices. Through the coaching process, I discovered that leaving the position of senior pastor was my choice, and rather than choose grief as the major paradigm through which I would experience my transition, I chose to focus on the power of choice. Grief is a natural part of the transition process and cannot be avoided. But, in accepting grief as part of the process, we have the choice for it not to be the major focus of the transition.

Most people have the power of choice in their life. No matter the situation, most of us have the power to choose, if nothing else, our response. In employment situations, one has the ability and the choice to leave on one's own terms. I realize that there are situations of forced terminations, layoffs, and other forms of leavings where it appears that a person does not have choice. I believe that if one prepares oneself, then even forced leavings can be a choice. We forget this truth: no matter what happens, we have the power of choice.

To exercise choice, one must make preparation through creative living. Creative living is a choice and involves maximum creativity in the four areas that I

---

26. Robert Creech, "Bowen Theory and Pastoral Transition," in *Family Systems Forum 12/3* (Fall 2010).

listed in the preceding sermon: financial, physical, vocational, and spiritual creativity. Since I detailed the four areas in the sermon itself, I would rather give you the life experience that taught me to be creative in the four areas in the hopes that it will inspire and encourage you to your own stories and creative living.

I learned to be financially creative because I decided that I wanted to retire. I remember going to the financial planner and announcing that I wanted to retire. The planner made this ominous statement that immediately cut into my exuberance: "Let's look at the numbers because the numbers do not lie." After consulting the numbers, she looked me squarely in the eye and told me that I did not have enough money to retire if I wanted to maintain my present lifestyle. Based upon the fact that in the early years of my ministry I neglected savings and retirement contributions, I would run out of money in a few years. Right there in the financial planner's office, I broke down into tears. I had worked all of these years and did not have enough to retire. In the next week, I met with the financial planner again and asked her if she could work with my wife and me and help us design a plan where I could retire. We worked together and designed a plan that would give me choice. I prepared myself to make the choice of retirement by creative financial planning. If you do not have a retirement plan, it is never too late or too early. Make the choice to get a financial plan because someone may say to you one day that the numbers do not lie.

Early in my ministry, I learned a valuable lesson about physical well-being, including diet, exercise, and preventive wellness. I went into my office and my desk was filled with pink message slips that my executive assistant left for me to respond to. I was emotionally on the edge and exhausted. The vast number of messages took me over and I almost emotionally and physically collapsed. I decided to go on a spiritual retreat and meet with a spiritual director. Upon arrival at the retreat center, I immediately met with the spiritual director. She was a nun of German descent and spoke in broken, almost unintelligible English. I only understood half of what she said to me. Despite our communication issues, I poured my heart out to her. And when I finished, I waited for her to give me profound truth from both the Scriptures and her spiritual experience that would change my life and heal my spirit. She listened intently, waited, paused, and thought carefully about what she was going to say. Then she said this to me: "You need a nap!" I said, "Excuse me!" She said, "Go upstairs and sleep as long as you want to and get up only when you feel like it, and we will talk some more." I was disappointed and said, "A nap?" I thought I needed more than that. I was highly insulted. I needed a word from the Lord through her. I had no idea that you could not hear from the Lord without rest.

For the first time in a very long time, I slept as long as I wanted to. I slept all day, and every time I thought about getting up, I thought about what she said—sleep until I felt like getting up. I got up after dinner, and after eating, I met with this graceful and gifted nun. She was right—I had needed a nap. And aside from all the deep spiritual issues that we talked about in the next few days, we developed an awareness of the physical body, including rest, diet, and exercise. We talked through self-care and preventative wellness and developed a plan. And while I have had ups and downs with the plan, over the whole thirty-one years of ministry, I have taken care of my body and health. I did so to be able to exercise the power of choice for as long as possible without the negligence of physical concerns and health limiting my life. I prepared myself to make the choice of retirement by creative physical and mental wellness. If you are reading this book, put it down and go take a nap.

Thirdly, one must exercise vocational creativity to place oneself in position to maintain the power of choice. I was preaching at a very popular and well-attended citywide Lenten series. After the service, I went downstairs to the waffle shop to have lunch, and sitting at the table was a professor of communications and rhetoric. Quickly, he dispensed with the niceties and said to me that I would be a natural to teach communications and rhetoric, and he was recruiting me as a student for his program. I dismissed it. I was overwhelmed as a pastor already. I did not have the time or the energy. I took his card, but with no intention to ever call. Well, he called me and took me to lunch. I politely declined the invitation to become part of the program.

I was invited back the next year to preach the same Lenten series. Again, I went down to the waffle shop to have lunch. The same professor was sitting at the table. Again he made the comment that I would be a natural to teach communications and rhetoric. At a follow-up lunch, he suggested that I take one class and see what would happen. From somewhere deep inside, maybe inside out, this time I readily agreed. I took one class and fell in love with communications and rhetoric. I subsequently graduated with a degree in communication and rhetoric. This degree would strategically position me in my life after pastoring a congregation. We must think carefully about where our lives will be when we are, for example, no longer pastoring a congregation. We must exercise vocational creativity and position ourselves beyond where we are at the present moment.

Finally, one must exercise spiritual creativity in order to maintain choice in one's life. In 1986, my wife and I went to the hospital to have our first daughter, Ashley Re Thomas. When Ashley Re came out of the womb, she had what we subsequently learned was a diaphragmatic hernia, which meant there was hole in her diaphragm, and her heart and lungs had grown together. She was fine when she breathed the liquid of the womb, but when she tried to breathe air, she went into crisis. My daughter lived nine hours and died on the operating table. The hardest thing that I ever had to do in my life was to walk into a hospital room and tell my wife that our daughter had died on the operating table. I could not form the words; the tears on my face told her, and we cried uncontrollably together.

The death was unplanned. As a matter of fact, the opposite was planned, with a decorated room, crib, and future dreams already completed. I was a pastor. We had served God faithfully, and this should not have happened to us because we were ministers of God. In the midst of my distress, I heard myself say, "Tragedy is available for everybody." And with that acknowledgment, I began reconstructing a deep and abiding hope in God, what I called hope for life. It took a tremendous amount of spiritual creativity to accept that there are no mistakes and no "bad" things. There is only the opportunity to grow, develop, and learn more about life and living. I remember the day that I quoted Genesis 1:31, where the text says, "God looked over everything that God had made and said that it was good." I realized that God did not say that it was perfect. There would be flaws, faults, and death in life. But despite tragedy, God said life was good, and I agreed. Spiritual creativity is the ability to take whatever happens in life and creatively work with it such that it accomplishes the good in one's life.

Grief is not the primary metaphor through which I view my transition. I operate primarily through the metaphor of choice and the releasing of my passion. The focus is on my choice and not on blaming, fighting, getting angry with those who resisted my leadership or presented roadblocks. Neither did I focus on the people that I loved and was leaving. I focused on the choice and will say more about the gratitude that I felt to all in one of the upcoming backstories.

11

DO YOU HAVE A TEACHABLE SPIRIT?

For you became sorrowful as God intended and so were not harmed in any way by us. Godly sorrow brings repentance that leads to salvation and leaves no regret, but worldly sorrow brings death. See what this godly sorrow has produced in you: what earnestness, what eagerness to clear yourselves, what indignation, what alarm, what longing, what concern, what readiness to see justice done. At every point you have proved yourselves to be innocent in this matter.

—2 CORINTHIANS 7:9B–11 NIV

In the fall of 1976, prior to entering seminary and exploring a call that would eventually lead to pastoral ministry, I worked as a security guard for the trading floor of the Chicago Mercantile Exchange from midnight to eight in the morning. There was not much activity to be concerned with, and after a week of absolute quiet, I decided to pass the time with a stack of books to read. The first book was Alex Haley's *The Autobiography of Malcolm X.* I read those four hundred or so pages, and when I got to the end of the book, the part where Malcolm X was assassinated at the Audubon Ballroom in New York City, I cried like a baby. Alone and by myself, I cried a river of tears on the trading floor of the Chicago Mercantile Exchange. In those pages, I had come to love

Malcolm X, and love was not too strong a word. Subsequently, I read everything I could get my hands on about Malcolm X and began to learn why I loved him so.

It is not simply because of the political and the revolutionary rhetoric that I love Malcolm X. I appreciate that he spoke up for African American people against racism, oppression, prejudice, and self-hatred, and for self-determination. He was insightful, gifted, and still continues to be relevant almost fifty years after his death. Because he was a human being, some things he said and did were right, and other things I did not agree with. At the core, I love him because he could be transformed. He was a dynamic and creative character. He was not static. He could change. He could grow. He could expand. He could stretch. He could enlarge. He could even go beyond the limits of Elijah Muhammad, whom he credits with saving his life. He could broaden, expand, and increase. He could go from Malcolm Little to Detroit Red to Malcolm X to El-Hajj Malik El-Shabazz. He had a teachable spirit.

Many people go through their lives being who they have always been, thinking what they have always thought, believing what they always believed, keeping the same friends they always kept, going to the same places they've always gone. Many people have never traveled, never been off the block, never been out of the city, never been out of their state, and never been out of the country. Many people have never been close to someone of another race, nation, culture, religion, political party, or sexual persuasion. Many people have never gone beyond their group. Many people have never stretched and have never expanded.

But, in my life, I want to grow. I want to stretch. I want to enlarge. I want to expand! I want to see! I want to experience! I want to feel and hear! I want to think in ways I've never thought before. I want to experience truths that I've never experienced before! I want to extend. I want to be transformed. I want a teachable spirit.

This is what I love about Malcolm X: he had a teachable spirit. A teachable spirit is a spirit that can be taught; a spirit that can change, grow, and expand; a spirit that is not satisfied with the status quo and that never tires of learning; a spirit that travels; a spirit that hungers for truth; a spirit that reads; a spirit that has dialogue, even with folks with whom one may not agree; a spirit that is expectant in pursuing new truth and new revelation. Malcolm X had a teachable spirit.

How does one get to possess a teachable spirit? How does one get this kind of hunger, this kind of thirst? How does one know that one has a teachable spirit? How does one live with this kind of fervor and this kind of zest for life and learning? We have to look at the situation in second Corinthians in the seventh chapter for hints about a teachable spirit.

Paul had a very contentious and rocky relationship with the church at Corinth. He started this church in the home of Chloe (see Acts 18). As was Paul's custom, he would get to a place, start a church, establish leadership, and then move on to the next place to start another church. He established the church in Corinth, raised up leadership, and then continued on his missionary journey to Macedonia.

When Paul got to Macedonia, he got word that the folk in Corinth were "cutting up" and "acting crazy" big time. We get some hints about their unspiritual behavior in a later letter that Paul wrote to them that we know as First Corinthians. In 1 Corinthians 3, some followed Paul, some followed Apollos, and some followed Peter. They were split up into divided factions with jealousy and quarreling, and as a result, Paul called them mere infants in Christ. In 1 Corinthians 5, we discover sexual immorality. A man had his father's wife (stepmother) as his own and nobody in the church got upset, and as a matter of fact the church was proud. Paul said that even pagans did not do that. In 1 Corinthians 6, believers were suing one another and taking one another to court for non-Christian judges to settle the matter. Paul asked if there were not spiritual people in the church who could judge the matter. Paul says the fact that they had lawsuits among them meant they were completely defeated. In 1 Corinthians 11, they were misusing and abusing the Lord's Supper. In 1 Corinthians 12, the tongue-speaking crowd considered themselves spiritually superior to everyone else. In 1 Corinthians 14, the worship service descended into chaos because everyone claimed the preeminence of his/her gift of the Spirit. Paul got word that they were acting like this and decided to send a few words of correction to them.

Paul sent them a letter that we have no record of. They got the letter from Paul and decided not to obey or repent. They sent a delegation back to Paul with a list of questions to which they wanted Paul to respond. The letter we know as 1 Corinthians is Paul's response to the questions that they wanted answered and a reiteration of what he had said in his earlier letter. They received the letter but didn't repent. They didn't have a teachable spirit. They sent another letter demanding that Paul respond to some more of their questions.

They were bold in their sin and arrogance, and as a result, unteachable. They criticized Paul and challenged his integrity. Paul decides that he's going to pay them a visit. Paul said many of the people in Corinth were doing much talking, but the kingdom of God was not a matter of talk, but a matter of power. In 1 Corinthians 4:20, Paul said, "I'm going to show up in town to see what power you have."

Well, after selling those "wolf tickets" about coming to town and challenging their power, Paul was delayed in Macedonia. When he didn't show up, the people got even more bold and aggressive against Paul. They called Paul flaky and double minded. They considered themselves waiting on him and ready for the confrontation with him. They accused Paul of being sometimes no and sometimes yes.

Paul hears this and sits down and writes what he calls a "sorrowful letter." Paul just lays into them and says what he wants to say and how he wants to say it. His patience is short and he does not pull back, but writes what he calls a sorrowful letter. A sorrowful letter is a letter that you write saying everything that you thought you wanted to say to tell a person off, and then you lick the envelope, put a stamp on it, put it in the mailbox, and as soon as it falls down the chute, you do everything that you can to reach down and snatch it back out, but it's too late. That's called a sorrowful letter.

A sorrowful letter is when you tell your boss everything you want to tell the boss and what the boss can do with the job. You let the boss have it with double barrels loaded. You hit the send button on the e-mail and you feel better for a short time. You go downstairs and get the mail and discover the large number of bills waiting for you in the mailbox. You head back upstairs to check to see if you can unsend the letter and you notice that the boss has already sent you a response and you are scared to open it. That's a sorrowful letter.

We have all written sorrowful letters. We have all learned that some of these letters you ought to sleep on. Some of these letters you ought to pray over. Some of these letters ought to wait. You ought not send them right after you've written them. The feelings are too raw and you run the risk of doing more harm than good.

Paul wrote this letter, and after he wrote it, he regretted it. Paul wanted to take it back. Was it too harsh? Would it push them away further? Well, the text says that when they got the letter, quite to Paul's surprise, they repented. I think we're ready for the text. Let's look at 2 Corinthians, the seventh chapter, beginning with the eighth verse:

> Even if I caused you sorrow by my letter, I don't regret it. Though I did regret it—I see that my letter hurt you but only for a little while—yet now I am happy, not because you were made sorry, but because your sorrow led you to repentance. For you became sorrowful as God intended and so were not harmed by us. Godly sorrow brings repentance that leads to salvation and leaves no regret, but worldly sorrow brings death. See what this godly sorrow has produced in you: what earnestness, what eagerness to clear yourselves, what indignation, what alarm, what longing, what concern, what readiness to see justice done.

They repented. To Paul's surprise, they repented. Paul was worried that his letter was too rough. He was worried, but they were not harmed in any way. In their repentance, we can see three elements that we can use to discern if we have a teachable spirit.

To have a teachable spirit, first, you must bow down to spiritual authority. There must be a person or several critical persons we call our spiritual mothers and our spiritual fathers. Somebody must explain to us. Somebody must disciple us. Somebody must mentor us. Somebody must show us the ropes. Somebody must expand our minds and our thinking. Somebody must challenge us. Somebody must love us. Somebody must reprove us. Somebody must rebuke us. Somebody must speak the truth in love to us! Nobody comes here as an instant Christian. Who is your spiritual mother and/or your spiritual father?

Let me ask the same question another way? Who can pull your chain? Who can tell you you're out of order? Who can tell you to cease and desist? We have people who cannot be put in check. We have Christians just like these Corinthians before they repented who cannot be put in spiritual check. We have ministers who will not submit to a pastor. We have choir members who won't give respect and authority to the minister of music. Some Christians are just like these Corinthians before they repented. To whom do you bow down in spiritual authority? Who can call you into spiritual accountability? Who can tell you, cease and desist!

The story of Harry Truman and General Douglas MacArthur illustrates this concept of accountability. Harry Truman was the president of the United States. MacArthur was a popular hero of World War II who was the commander of United Nations forces fighting in the Korean War. MacArthur made statements that contradicted the president's policies. Truman sent word: "Cease and desist." But, because MacArthur was popular, he refused. Truman relieved MacArthur of his command. And the story has it that Truman sent a private to snatch the bars off the uniform of General MacArthur.

What I am suggesting is that God will say cease and desist. If you refuse, God will send an usher to snatch the bars off the robe of the pastor or your Christian uniform. You must submit to spiritual authority if you are going to have a teachable spirit.

Second, to have a teachable spirit, you must be able to tolerate, every now and then, a sorrowful letter. Sometimes God will send you a sorrowful letter for the purpose of correction. Sorrowful letters cause great pain, and it takes great pain to change and grow. Kahlil Gibran says that pain is the breaking of the shell that encloses our understanding. Pain is often the method by which we gain new insight. What I have learned is that I do not do much with what I hear until the pain of staying the way that I am is greater than the pain of change. People who have not had enough of the pain are, as Edwin H. Friedman said, invulnerable to insight. People change when they get tired of hurting. Prior to new insight, a sorrowful letter must come that indicates our behavior misses the mark.

Every now and then God will send a sorrowful letter to your address deep in your heart. I have been given occasional sorrowful letters all of my life. Upon receipt of the sorrowful letter, you have a choice to make. Which is worse, the pain of change or the pain of staying the same? God will allow you to suffer the consequences to help you make up your mind. The choice is change or misery. Pain is inevitable, but misery is optional. Misery is what you add to pain when you refuse to change. If you get a sorrowful letter, repent quickly. If you get a sorrowful letter, change quickly, because not changing leads to misery, which is spiritual death. Change is called godly sorrow in the text and godly sorrow leads to salvation. The refusal to change, what the text calls worldly sorrow, leads to misery and death. Paul sent a letter and made the Corinthian church sorry. But their godly sorrow led to repentance and salvation.

Finally, to have a teachable spirit is to welcome reconciliation, the beneficial outcome of godly sorrow. Reconciliation is one of the most beautiful experiences in human life. Paul's letter had been received in a spirit of humility, a willingness to follow God's will, and it produced repentance and reconciliation. Look closely at the specific words that Paul uses in verse 11 of our text. The letter produces in them "earnestness" to clear themselves and their name of any blame. It produced in them "indignation" at the sinful actions of persons who violated the Scriptures and who disrespected Paul. It produced in them "alarm" over their behavior and its effects on themselves and others. It produced "longing" and "concern," which is affection for Paul and a longing for him to visit in person. Lastly, it produced "readiness to see justice done" by the punishment of offenders and a promotion of a community of people living in right relationship with God, each other, and Paul.

Reconciliation is one of the most beautiful and healing experiences in human living. Verse 11 suggests that reconciliation is in us deeper than division; that love is in us deeper than hate; that peace is deeper in us than violence; that forgiveness is in us deeper than lack of forgiveness; that mercy is in us deeper than judgment. The world is filled with division, hate, violence, and lack of forgiveness, but reconciliation will have the last word. It is the promise of the cross and the resurrection of Jesus Christ that evil will not win. In 2 Corinthians 5:19 Paul says that reconciliation will have the last word: God was in Christ reconciling the world to Godself . . . and has committed to us the message of reconciliation. In Christ, reconciliation will have the last word.

Reconciliation is one of the most healing experiences in life; that which was broken is now restored. Reconciliation is why we love the story of healing between the father and the son in Luke 15. What is a more beautiful verse in the entire Bible than Luke 15:32, "We had to celebrate and be glad, because this brother of yours was dead and is alive again; he was lost and is found"? Paul exhibits the same joy and enthusiasm in 2 Corinthians 7:11 as is reported in Luke 15:32. Paul was overjoyed at the possibility of a new relationship. Reconciliation is one of the most beautiful and healing experiences in human living. The truth of the matter is that, to have reconciliation, you must have a teachable spirit. Do you have a teachable spirit?

THE BACKSTORY

As part of leaving well, it is important for the transitioning pastor to take an objective assessment of his/her strengths, challenges, and leadership style in the departing ministry context. I had been the senior pastor of Mississippi Boulevard Christian Church for thirteen years and accomplished many wonderful and amazing things, and also made various mistakes and suffered numerous self-inflicted wounds. In many church contexts, celebrations of the transition of the pastor are filled with the joys, strengths, and the beneficial achievements of the pastor. Where possible, these celebrations should be positive and encouraging, if, in fact, the festivities are true and genuine. My suggestion is that a private forum with an atmosphere of trust be created, for an honest discussion of the strengths and challenges of *both* the pastor and the congregation. Let me reiterate: the purpose of this session is not venting, conflict resolution, or uttering frustration, unhappiness, or disappointment. It is the opportunity for both departing pastor and congregation to be helpful to one another with mutual learning and insights necessary for each to be successful in their journeys ahead. Not to create such a forum is to miss an opportunity for both to grow. Sometimes the discussion might feel like a "sorrowful letter," but as the Corinthians learned, sorrowful letters are an opportunity to grow and experience closure and reconciliation. I wanted an objective assessment of the strengths and challenges of my ministry and the places that I could still grow. I also wanted closure and reconciliation.

Initially, we hired Carl George to help us assess our attendance at the Midtown campus, but his consultation presented the opportunity for an independent, outside person to receive feedback from the congregation and myself, and as part of a broader report to the church, help the church and myself discern our strengths and challenges. Carl George was exactly the person to function as an outside observer and potentially offer a sorrowful letter to both the congregation and the senior pastor.

George's methodology was to meet with a number of different leadership and ministry groups in the church in order to gain various kinds of input. He met with nine groups and did several interviews with individuals. He talked to over a hundred people, what he called "pulsing them, being present with them, taking questions from them, and sharing various insights." Ultimately, he had no agenda, but simply asked people to define their concerns and state the questions that they had. After the meetings and interviews, based upon the expression of common concerns and questions, the leading of the Holy Spirit, and George's expertise and experience in church growth, a picture began to emerge that he reported to the congregation and the senior pastor.

In George's initial report, he made this recommendation among several others: "provide staff with the support of a consultation that examines their morale and operational model." In his consultation, he had picked up tension and concern from the staff. I fully supported the implementation of this recommendation, and we quickly followed up with the additional consultation. It was in the consultation with the staff that I received direct and excellent feedback relative to the strengths and challenges of my leadership style.

George discerned much strength in my leadership. He talked most of all about my integrity. There was no moral fault found in my thirteen years as the pastor of MBCC and the standard of spiritual excellence and leadership I provided. He commented that my soul was made of "titanium" because I had weathered some of the most vicious attacks on the church that he had ever seen anywhere. Graciously, he commented that my perseverance, faithfulness, and tenacity were legendary and were worthy of further study as an asset for pastors. There were more strengths that he shared, such as my preaching ministry, communication skills, depth and clarity of thinking, and trust among the congregation and staff. While certainly not meant to be an exhaustive list or the central aim of the report, he gave remarkably affirmative and positive feedback.

In my personal interview with George, I said that I once heard a trainer say that if there were problems in the staff, "the breadcrumbs always lead to the door of the CEO." In other words, the fact that he found tension in the staff meant that I, as the leader, the chief of staff, had some burden of responsibility as to why things were the way they were. I asked him not to pull any punches because I have a teachable spirit and I could not grow without the truth.

He did not pull punches and the latter part of the report came to me as a sorrowful letter. This is what he said about the challenges in my leadership style:

> Temperamentally, Pastor Thomas does not naturally insist on his own way, does not power up on individuals who assert their agendas, wishes to play as a member of a team, and seeks peaceful outcomes to problems. He hopes that staff and lay leaders will play nice, even though both have a track record for misbehavior. His pastoral impulses have not served him well as a supervisor of staff, because he sees the potential in errant staff members and delays disciplining or expelling them, when a seasoned manager would put them on probation and then terminate their employment if their attitudes and performance did not improve. . . . This pastoral impulse is accompanied by a reluctance to confront. Another pastoral leader would not tolerate fraternizing between staff and lay leaders, because such relationships lead to breakdowns in staff/supervisor relationships. If an administrator tolerates disgruntled staff taking their gripes and peeves to board members, he will not be able to provide clarity in directing staff energy.

This was a sorrowful letter. He spoke the truth. It was nothing that I had not heard or known. The truth is that I had been grappling with this for some time. I could not leave without hearing this part of the truth. I did not get angry, upset, or depressed. I did not beat myself up or slip into wondering what I could have done or should have done. It was simply feedback that I had the choice to learn from and do something about. I decided upon godly sorrow. I received the information and decided to make some course corrections. I wanted to be reconciled to God and to the congregation. I wanted to forgive and be forgiven. I wanted to know and be known, or as a friend of mine said to me in so many words, "We do not know each other until we know and accept each other's painful faults and flaws."

I believe that this kind of truth is our only hope. I want to accept the truth and grow from it. I want a teachable spirit.

This is my prayer for people, all congregations, and clergy everywhere:

May God grant us all the grace to grow, stretch, expand, extend, and enlarge from the sorrowful letters that we receive from the hand of the Lord. May we have godly sorrow.

NO HURT LIKE A CHURCH HURT

Therefore, as we have opportunity, let us do good to all people,
especially to those who belong to the family of believers.

—GALATIANS 6:10 NIV

Several years ago, I had lunch with a woman who had been a pastor's wife for many years and a wonderful preacher in her own right. The pastor, her husband, had passed away, and we had a chance to really talk in my attempt to minister to her in her grief. She had major bitterness and resentment toward the church for all that she and her husband had gone through in his service to them as their pastor. Wanting to make the conversation positive, I asked her: What have you learned from your years of experience in ministry? I was not ready for the answer that she gave. She said, "Ain't no hurt like a church hurt." Do you know what she means? Have you ever been hurt in church? Has someone you loved ever been hurt in church? Do you know what she is talking about? Would you agree, ain't no hurt like a church hurt?

Someone here might disagree and suggest that ain't no hurt like a divorce hurt. Or ain't no hurt like an affair hurt. Ain't no hurt like a loss of spouse hurt. Ain't no hurt like a layoff hurt. Ain't no hurt like a bankruptcy hurt. And I know all of those experiences hurt deeply and are not to be trivialized. I want to argue that a church hurt is the worst of all hurts. Why? Because the church is the place where you expect to get help and healing for all the other hurts of life. The church is the place where you bring the divorce hurt, the layoff hurt, the affair hurt, and the bankruptcy hurt. When you are hurt in church, you run the risk of having no place to bring your hurt, save directly to God. And many people have difficulty going directly to God when they have seen the church as the mediator of God's presence and have been hurt in the church. There is no hurt like a church hurt.

I asked a good friend why there are no hurts like church hurts, and my friend told me that it had to do with the standard of moral value that we preach, profess, and proclaim in the church. Maybe it's all this God talk about love, compassion, peace, and mercy, about following Jesus, and all the "love your enemy" language. We say on a regular basis, "Forgive us as we forgive others"; "bless those who spitefully use you"; "pray for those who curse you." We quote Scripture about what Jesus did, how Jesus acted, how Jesus loved, how Jesus forgave, how Jesus touched, how Jesus listened, how Jesus was patient, and how Jesus was merciful. Though Jesus engaged plenty of conflict, Jesus lived a higher moral standard, and we often profess that we are trying to be like Jesus. In the church, we offer so much Jesus talk, and sometimes there is so little Jesus behavior in the church. And our talk sets up expectations that we will act like Jesus, and when people do not act like Jesus in the church, it hurts all the more. Ain't no hurt like a church hurt.

We expect a "dog-eat-dog" competition, cutthroat behavior in relationships, and every person for themselves in the world. People often say and feel, "But maybe if I just come to church, I might find something different than what's in the world, like love, compassion, mercy, gentleness, and forgiveness." When people get judgment, harsh words, and a putdown, hurt is how they name their disappointment. When the church falls short, when the church looks like every other human institution, it is especially disappointing because we expect different, higher, and better in the church.

Across the years I've seen a lot of hurt in church. Some of the hurts in the churches that I've seen are not the fault of the church. Some people are unreasonable. Some people are hypersensitive. Some people are immature. Some people are manipulative. Some people want what they want and will do whatever it takes to get what they want. And, when they don't get their way, then they have hurt feelings. I've seen people who are as aggressive as hell, hurting people, wounding people to get their way, and then when you call them out, all of a sudden they get hurt—like you really hurt their feelings. Why is it that the most belligerent people have the most sensitive feelings when they're called on their belligerence? Not all of the hurts in church are the fault of the church. Sometimes it is the fault of the individual.

However, on the other hand, I've seen innocent, well-meaning people who simply want to serve God out of their heart get mauled, body slammed, chewed up, and spit out in the church. One of my staff members coined this phrase: "Church is a contact sport." He meant that in church there will be personality conflicts, hidden agendas, sabotage, land mines, passive aggression, division, factions, etc., and everyone will have to come in contact with it, engage it, wrestle with it, deal with it, and by God's grace overcome it. When you come into church, make sure you have your pads on because church is a contact sport.

I've always tried to prepare people for the reality of the church. But, no matter how I try, sooner or later a person has to come to terms with that fact that "ain't no hurt like a church hurt." The road to maturity in church is that you have to go through a church hurt or two. You have to go through a church hurt to get to maturity. I do know that there are people who, once they face the reality of the church hurt, go back to the pew, listen to the preacher and the choir, and say, "I am not interested in the behind-the-scenes stuff of church." People will come to church to receive, but they will quickly leave out the front door. They are afraid that if they come close to hurt in church, rather than relieve their hurt, the church will add to the burden of hurt that they already carry. Ain't no hurt like a church hurt.

Some of what causes hurt in the church is the utilization of the principles of Machiavelli. In his book *The Prince*, Machiavelli sets forth tactics to win political battles. He said that the end justifies the means. He meant the end is the goal that you want to achieve, and you can behave by any means necessary to get to your end. Morality can be suspended to get to your goal because the end justifies the means. Machiavelli said, "Since love and fear can hardly exist together, if we must choose between them, it's far safer to be feared than to be loved." Leaders must diligently and intentionally make sure that they are feared.

Tell me how both of these fit with Jesus, Christian fellowship, and the Sermon on the Mount? How do they fit with the Bible? It might be that I am a purist, with an ideal that has no basis in reality, but I believe the principles of Machiavelli are not for the church. I am not sure that the maxim "the end justifies the means" works well in the church because I do not believe you can use unspiritual methods to get to spiritual ends. It is impossible to hate your way to love or lie your way to truth. It is very difficult to use unspiritual means to get to spiritual ends. Not everything that Machiavelli says fits in the church. Paul said in 2 Corinthians 10: "the weapons of our warfare are not carnal," meaning, not of the world and not of Machiavelli.

When we use the tactics of Machiavelli, and then use the spiritual language of the Christian faith, the result is "ain't no hurt like a church hurt." Spiritual language as a thin veneer over Machiavellian tactics makes people hurt all the more. People are desperate for people who will walk their talk. They say, "If I could just find somebody who believes the Bible! If I could just find somebody who lives what he/she preaches, prays, and sings." Didn't the 1952 Nobel Peace Prize winner Albert Schweitzer once say that he would become a Christian if he ever saw one?

Paul says to us in the Galatians text, *Do good to all people; especially to the household of faith.* Some commentators rightly propose that Paul is talking about money in verses 6–10 and I will quickly give you some of the overwhelming evidence. First, in verse 6, Paul is clearly referring to sharing financial resources with the teacher when he says, "the one who receives instruction in the word must share all good things with the instructor." In verse 7, Paul says that a person reaps what he/she sows. Paul is referring to the use of money to build the spiritual life rather than the sinful nature. Also, this is a proverb that Paul uses in 2 Corinthian 6:9 to encourage generous giving. The phrase "do good to all" in verse 10 is a euphemism for giving alms. Finally, giving for the collection of the Jerusalem poor is important to Paul as a result of the Jerusalem council (Gal. 2:10), and wherever he went he talked to the churches about giving to Jerusalem.

One commentator sums up the evidence by suggesting that three uses of money are mentioned:

> 1) the support of the teacher in a Christian congregation, 2) the use of money to build up the life of the Spirit rather than feed the flesh, and 3) the spending of money to help others, especially Christians. The principle that ties all three points together is that enunciated in the proverb: reaping is in proportion to sowing. Thus, one will get out of their effort what they put in.[27]

There is no question that Paul is talking about money in this text, specifically the use of money to build the spiritual life.

Though we could apply this text to Christian behavior with money, I would like to make the focus broader than money. Just as we declare a war on cancer, I am declaring a war on church hurt. I want to apply this text as a balm, a salve, as an antibiotic against church hurt: "therefore do good to all people, especially those who belong to the family of believers," that is, especially those in church.

I want to suggest an ethic or spiritual principle to minimize and resolve the amount of hurt in church. I received this spiritual principle in a time of retreat and silence before God. After intense Scripture reading, prayer, and meditation, it became clear what I wanted, really: I wanted to please God and do the right thing in all relationships. From that revelation, I adopted this as the personal mission statement of my ministry to the church: to mold the moral character of the church such that there is in the heart of every person a passionate desire to please God and do the right thing in all relationships. I began to preach sermon series, teach Bible classes, train in meetings, and encourage the congregation to adopt this mantra—"Do the right thing in all relationships." When we have an intense and passionate desire to please God and do the right thing in all relationships, it minimizes church hurt.

---

27. Frank E. Gaebelein, *The Expositor's Bible Commentary* (Grand Rapids: Zondervan, 1986), 503.

My passionate desire to please God and do the right thing in all relationships has kept my marriage together for thirty-six years. In my marriage, my goal is to please God first. And if I please God, then I know that I will love and please my wife. There have been critical times of conflict, trouble, and disagreement in our relationship when I have had to ask: Is what you just did or said pleasing to God? Is God pleased with how you are treating your wife? And if God was not pleased, then I apologized and changed. If we change what we are doing that is destructive to the relationship, then the relationship goes better and there is less hurt. Let me give you an example of what I mean.

I had a couple come in for a counseling session and they argued back and forth. It got so intense right in front of me that if they had had a knife or a gun, somebody would have probably been hurt. I tried all my counseling skills and what I had traditionally done in working with couples for thirty-one years. Every time I tried to elevate the conversation above bickering, they would go back to fighting. Finally, I said, "This behavior is an affront to Jesus Christ. Both of you are claiming to be Christians and you are acting like this." She said, like she had heard it all before, "Blah, blah, blah, blah." Despite my anger, I remained calm, "Could you explain to me how Jesus might be pleased with what you just said?" Then he said, "Get her, pastor! You know she's got a mouth. Now you see what I'm going through." And I said, "Now tell me how God is pleased with what you just said. As a matter of fact, if you want to see me again, you both will have to agree to a homework assignment." I told them go home and get a piece of paper. Spend some time with God and answer these questions: *Is God pleased with how I'm behaving? Do I have a desire to be pleasing to God?* I told them that if both of them did not have answers to these questions, then helping them was beyond my skill set and I would refer them to someone else. They both came back with answers and it got better. It was not a total fix to their relationship, and much work lay ahead, but it was a positive beginning. I am suggesting that we minimize hurt when we have an intense desire to please God and do the right thing in all relationships.

When we have an intense desire to please God and do the right thing in all relationships, then we do good to everybody—especially the household of faith. Paul is emphasizing the point that we should especially do good to the "family of believers," those who are related to us by believing in the Lord Jesus Christ. He suggests this relationship should transcend all others. This is not to neglect anyone who is not a Christian, it is to indicate that one especially goes out of one's way, one tries extra hard and is extra good to those in the household of faith. Paul is suggesting that we be especially concerned with the spiritual welfare of those of the household of faith because ain't no hurt like a church hurt. You heal people by doing good.

I translate doing good in this text as good deeds that amount to taking care of one another. When we do the right thing in all relationships, we take care of one another. When we take care of one another, we are like minded toward each other and there are no divisions. When we take care of one another, we share and distribute excess. There may be someone you know in need of a car to provide for the family, and we have members that have an extra car in their driveway or garage that they are not even using. Take care of one another. Do you know I have members with furniture in storage that pay a monthly storage bill on furniture they hope to use, might use, can't use, and at the same time we have people who are leasing or buying furniture on charge cards to have furniture? The word says share your excess. Take care of one another by sharing and distributing your excess, especially to the members of the household of faith. Take care of one another. Do good to all—especially in the household of faith. Come together around the Word of God. Receive each other to the glory of God. Do good to all—especially in the household of faith. Remember, ain't no hurt like a church hurt.

THE BACKSTORY

There are far too many people who come out of paid and volunteer positions in church ministry hurt, wounded, angry, and bitter. When a good friend of mine left a ministry position several weeks ago, I told him that he got out reasonably whole, considering that I know many who are offended, injured, upset, and deeply stung by the ministry experience. I did not want to leave the pastoral ministry suffering and with unhealed scars. I did not want to leave hurt, wounded, angry, and bitter. I kept these thoughts uppermost in my mind. I said to myself over and over again that no one makes us feel anything, and as a result, our feelings are our own choice and responsibility. I exercised my power of choice and decided, in my leaving, despite the church hurts I felt and experienced, they would not be my focus. I would be an advocate for positive and constructive change to help the congregation, staff, and the new pastor have the best chance at success. Being an advocate for positive and constructive change pleased God; therefore, the third aspect of leaving well is to be an advocate for a positive transition to help the congregation, staff, and the new pastor succeed.

I find it easier to be positive in the midst of transition when I am not a victim and when I exercise the power of choice in my life. The power of choice allows me to take full responsibility for my emotional well-being and not transition wounded and bitter. I will not rehash all that I have already said so far about the power of choice. Suffice it to say that a person who cultivates choice in his/her life has less of a chance of being bitter and wounded. Choice shifts one from victim and conflict energy and gives one power over one's life and emotions. What I want to share in this backstory are practical strategies that I adopted to operate from within the power of choice and be an advocate for positive and constructive change in my transition.

Before I begin to share strategies, I acknowledge that there are many models for pastoral transition, given the many ministry contexts and congregational polities. My context is that I was the fifth pastor of a ninety-one-year-old congregation. My thirteen-year ministry meant that I was not the founding pastor and did not function like a founding pastor. I did not have the capital to pick or heavily influence the choice of my successor. Not that I wanted to, but the polity of the congregation was clear that the church would pick its successor, and any influence that I had was informal. I was fine with all of that because my goal was to manage my own life and anxiety and leave the congregation to manage theirs. We were mature people in a relationship and could respect each other's boundaries and space. If they needed my help, they would ask for it, and I would help if asked.

Initially, I worked with the leadership team to develop a transition plan that would activate the moment that I made the official announcement of my retirement to church leadership and the congregation. I helped shape the process that led to the formation of a transition team to manage the affairs of the transition. However, once the team got to the point of the search, and especially when candidates were being considered, I stepped back so as not to interfere in any way with their work. I read a quote by Edwin H. Friedman that bolstered my thinking in this area: "Certainly, trying to influence the selection process of one's successor is 'akin' to trying to choose a mate for one's child or trying to nullify his or her choice."[28] At Friedman's and my wife's advice, as my first strategy to transition well, I did not attempt to influence the selection process of the next pastor.

Secondly, at every opportunity, I expressed the utmost confidence in the congregation, the staff, and in the church leadership. I believe that my leadership and tenure had strengthened, matured, and developed the leadership, congregation, and staff to be able to handle my leaving. As a matter of fact, the certainty of my eventual leaving motivated me to empower, develop, and entrust to the congregation and staff the responsibility for the ministry. I did not build a personality-driven ministry that could not survive my departure. I remember that one preacher preached on a Sunday morning when I was absent. In the follow-up conversation, he told me that things ran smoothly, and the church felt like a well-oiled machine, whether I was there or not. I said to him that people do when you are gone what they do when you are there. If people stand around and watch you do ministry while you are there, they will stand around and watch while you are gone. If people are partners and share ministry with you while you are around, then they will do what they have always been doing while you are not around. The church was more ready for my leaving than they knew. I had been preparing them for this for thirteen years. Leaving well has to do with preparing people for the transition years before leaving, and then expressing utmost confidence that they can and will do what you trained them to do.

Next, I apologized to the church for my shortcomings as a leader. I admitted to the church that I made many mistakes, and there are many things I would have liked to have done differently. At every point, I had no malicious intent to anyone. I did what I thought was best for the church and what I thought would please God. I told them that I forgave everybody and anyone that had done anything wrong to me. If I had conducted myself in a manner that was not spiritual, then I asked forgiveness from anyone whom I wronged. I wanted to wipe the slate clean. I told them that I ran out of gas at the end. I told them that I had been a pastor for thirty-one years of my life, and at the end of my pastoral ministry, I did

---

28. Edwin H. Friedman, *Generation to Generation: Family Process in Church and Synagogue* (New York: Guilford Press, 2011), 259.

not have the energy to take the church to the next level of growth and ministry. One of the indicators as to how I knew it was time to move on was that I did not think that the energy would come back with rest or a sabbatical. The passion was gone. Who I was now in my life did not align with what I was doing, and I felt the lack of energetic engagement. It is important to be honest with the church, admit shortcomings, forgive and ask forgiveness, and tell them the truth as to why you are leaving.

Fourthly, I reminded them of what a great church they were, and how I was blessed to be their senior pastor. I thanked each of them for their support of my leadership. When my leadership was under severe trial, they stayed with me and supported me. I thanked them for staying with me through the hard times. I thanked them for supporting my wife and family. I told them that we had done some amazing things because of their gifts, talents, and skills. Together, we met challenges, and, while there were too many accomplishments to list given time constraints, I could see that the spiritual maturity of the church, and mine too, was much better and stronger. I told them that I was leaving because God provided the place in my life where opportunity met passion. The opportunity to be a homiletics professor and open a preaching center was God's hand co-partnering with me to create the life that I wanted to live. It was an opportunity for me to live out my passion. I told them that I was grateful to God for each and every one of them and that I would never forget them. I would always remember their generosity and patience with me. Gratefulness was the overwhelming emotion in my closing months with them.

As part of my gratefulness, I pronounced a blessing over the church and the people. In my final congregational meeting, I pronounced this benediction from Acts 20:32 (MSG):

Now I'm turning you over to God, our marvelous God whose gracious Word can make you into what God wants you to be and give you everything you could possibly need in this community of holy friends.

part four

RELEASING THE CHOICE

✦ 13 ✦

THEY DID NOT INQUIRE OF THE LORD

"This bread of ours was warm when we packed it at home on the day we left to come to you. But now see how dry and moldy it is. And these wineskins that we filled were new, but see how cracked they are. And our clothes and sandals are worn out by the very long journey." The Israelites sampled their provisions but did not inquire of the LORD. —JOSHUA 9:12–14 NIV

How many critical decisions do we make in our lives and do not bother to ask God? There are people who change jobs, change cities, change their marital status, change houses, change churches, change schools, and change relationships and do not ask God about it. Are you facing some critical decision today? Are you considering a change? Let's look at what happens when you do not inquire of the Lord.

Here's the preamble to our scripture text: God spoke to Moses with signs and wonders to lead the people out of bondage from Egypt. When they are out of Egypt, and in the wilderness, Moses sends twelve spies to view the Promised Land. Ten spies come back and say that the land is great, but the people are like giants, and they recommend that Israel not attempt to take the land. Two of the spies, Joshua and Caleb, say to the people, "The Lord is with us. Do not be afraid of them." The people side with the report of the ten, and seek to kill Moses, Aaron, Joshua, and Caleb. God intervenes, and declares that based upon their faithlessness they will wander in the wilderness for forty years.

Almost forty years later, Moses leads the people to the edge of the Promised Land. Moses can see the Promised Land, but cannot enter into it. Moses dies, and Joshua, who served as a lieutenant to Moses, becomes the leader. Joshua devises a plan to conquer the Promised Land. He decides to overpower the center, march north, and finally come down to the south. Joshua's plan is working to perfection, and he defeats Jericho in Joshua 5–6 and Ai in chapter 8.

In chapter 9, verses 1–2 of our text, when all the kings west of the Jordan hear about the victories of Joshua and Israel, they decide to come together to fight against Joshua. They form an alliance so that Israel would no longer be able to conquer one city at a time. The alliance is made up of the Hittites, Amorites, Canaanites, Perizzites, Hivites, and Jebusites. They wage conventional war against Joshua and Israel.

In verses 3-6, after hearing about the defeat of Jericho and Ai, the Gibeonites decided on a different approach, a shrewd and ingenious plan. Rather than fight Joshua and Israel, they decide to trick Joshua into a treaty with them. They send out envoys whose donkeys were loaded with worn-out sacks and old wineskins, cracked and mended. The men put worn and patched sandals on their feet and wear old clothing. Their bread is dry and moldy. They go to Joshua and the men of Israel and say, "We have come from a distant country; make a treaty with us."

Now, the men of Israel are suspicious. In verse 7, the Israelites say to them, "Perhaps you live near us. How then can we make a treaty with you?" Let me give you a hint. If the Israelites were suspicious, why didn't they inquire of the Lord? They had doubts and uncertainty about the validity of these men's claims. Why not ask God? If you are not sure, why not ask God? Will somebody ask God?

In verse 8, the Gibeonites quickly say, "We are your servants." In other words, do not ask any hard questions, we will make your life easy and comfortable. Joshua asks this time, "Who are you and where do you come from?" In verses 9–13, they give an extended explanation of what they have already said to the leaders:

Your servants have come from a very distant country because of the fame of the Lord your God. For we have heard reports of him: all that he did in Egypt, and all that he did to the two kings of the Amorites east of the Jordan—Sihon king of Heshbon, and Og king of Bashan, who reigned in Ashtaroth. And our elders and all those living in our country said to us, "Take provisions for your journey; go and meet them and say to them, 'We are your servants; make a treaty with us.'" This bread of ours was warm when we packed it at home on the day we left to come to you. But now see how dry and moldy it is. And these wineskins that we filled were new, but see how cracked they are. And our clothes and sandals are worn out by the very long journey.

Another hint: Will somebody please talk to the Lord? Will somebody call on the name of the Lord? Will somebody call a prayer meeting? Will somebody fast and pray and seek the will of God about this matter? Both Joshua and the men of Israel have doubts; why don't they take their doubts to the Lord?

The text says in verse 14 that the men of Israel "sampled their provisions," but they did not inquire of the Lord. They checked to see if what the Gibeonites said about the condition of their food, clothing, and sandals was true. They checked the physical reality, but they did not check with the One who sees beyond appearances and physical reality to the spiritual reality. They did not consult the Lord. Nobody asked God about it.

In verse 15, Joshua made a treaty with them and the leaders of Israel ratified the treaty by an oath. And the Gibeonites' ruse worked, because the Israelites did not inquire of the Lord. Some of us can learn from this; if you have a decision today, you had better ask God about it. You had better inquire of the Lord. We can learn a tremendous amount from Joshua and Israel in this text. Do not do anything without inquiring of the Lord. Make sure you take everything to the Lord in prayer.

We do many things in church and we do not consult God. Can I name a few? We ordain deacons, trustees, board members, spiritual officers, and leaders in the church and do not consult the Lord. In other words, we put people in leadership positions based on "sampling their provisions" and do not ask God about it. We build buildings and facilities and do not consult the Lord. We call pastors to lead the church and do not consult the Lord. We use unspiritual means to secure the funds needed for the ministry and do not inquire of the Lord. We sing songs, pray prayers, and preach sermons and have not inquired of the Lord. And the whole time, we are using spiritual language, claiming that the Lord said this and the Lord said that. Has anybody really inquired of the Lord? Has anybody asked God? Can it be said of us what was said of the Israelites: we did not inquire of the Lord?

Let me warn you: like Joshua and Israel, the enemy will not come upon you with the same tricks and maneuvers. The enemy will not always attack you by frontal attack. The kings west of the Jordan formed an alliance and attacked Joshua and Israel in the conventional manner. But the enemy will come in even more creative and deceptive ways than the last time you confronted the enemy. Sometimes the enemy will come as a wolf dressed up in sheep's clothing. In 2 Corinthians 11:14, the Bible says that Satan will dress himself up like an angel of light. The enemy will dress up in things that look almost spiritual and if you have not asked God about it, then you will be deceived. Has anybody inquired of the Lord? Has anybody asked God?

Why don't we consult the Lord? We drift in our prayer life and our devotional life. We drift in our Bible study life. We think that we know what we are doing, and we do not need God. We neglect our spiritual life and our spiritual sensibilities become dull. And when our spiritual sensibilities become dull, so does our spiritual discernment. And before we know it, we have made a treaty with the enemy that allows him to live in our midst. And we realize that we did not inquire of the Lord.

The enemy does not always force his way into the camp. We make agreements and invite the enemy in. We go out and make covenants and treaties, like buying cars and houses we cannot afford, and taking vacations that we have to purchase on credit. We spend beyond our means and find ourselves in over our heads financially, and if we are honest about it, we are the ones who signed for the debt. We signed the treaty that allowed the debt enemy to reside amongst us. Nobody asked God, but we signed a steep mortgage. Nobody asked God, but we bought a pricey new car. We went lavish and expensive and blew up our budget to impress people, but has anybody inquired of the Lord? Has anybody asked God?

Don't we know the role of the Holy Spirit is to guide us into all truth? In John 14:26, Jesus promises a "comforter," which is the Holy Spirit. The role of the Holy Spirit is to comfort us, that is, come alongside us for aid, help, guidance, instruction, and revelation in all truth. The Holy Spirit is one who encourages, uplifts, and refreshes, who intercedes on our behalf as an advocate in court. The Holy Spirit is our counselor. With the Holy Spirit available, why don't we inquire of the Lord? Don't we know that the Holy Spirit will show us the truth in all things? But we do not consult the Lord.

Soon after Joshua and the Israelites make the treaty, they find out what they have done. In verses 16–18, they realize that they have been deceived. Three days later, they find out that they had made a treaty with the Gibeonites, their next door neighbors. Scarcely had the treaty been concluded that they discovered that they had been deceived. In our everyday language, this is known as "buyer's remorse." I remember when we bought our first house. We had been renting a place, and were very used to paying rent on a one-bedroom apartment. We saved our money and got our first mortgage. I started feeling bad when we signed all those papers at the mortgage company. We got the truck and moved the furniture from the apartment to the house, and as soon as we got all that furniture loaded off the truck, I thought about that big monthly house note, and I got sick. I thought about the fact that I would have to pay that amount for thirty years. I was in the bed for three days suffering from buyer's remorse, worried, stressed, and not sure I had done the right thing. Why didn't I take it slower? Why did I sign my life away? Had I asked God about it? The only thing that got me well was that my father came over and told me that he knew I was sick from worry. He came alongside for comfort and told me that we had a history of making good decisions and the house was a good decision. We had done well. At his word, I felt better. Joshua and the Israelites made a deal and were sick about it. They had not inquired of the Lord.

Joshua went out with fighting men three days journey to Gibeonite cities to confront and kill the Gibeonites, but could not attack because the Israelites had sworn an oath by the Lord, the God of Israel. When they returned, in the business meeting, the whole assembly grumbled against the leaders. They asked Joshua and the leaders, how did we get into this? How is it that God says the entire land is ours and yet you make a treaty and part of the land cannot be ours? In verse 19, the leaders tried to explain themselves, but they did not admit the truth—they had not inquired of the Lord. Instead, they came up with a plan in verse 20. They decided to let the Gibeonites live, but the Gibeonites would be wood-cutters and water carriers for the entire Israelite community. It was a good compromise. They could keep the treaty and the community could get the benefit of servants. It was a good solution and the people were satisfied. But, is it just me or did anybody notice that, again, they did not inquire of the Lord? I do not read in the text where it says that God told them to allow the Gibeonites to be woodcutters and water carriers. The Israelites found a solution, but I wonder if they made the same mistake: they did not inquire of the Lord.

My real concern is this: it's a good solution, but is it God's solution? Good solutions are the ones that we come up with to make a bad decision into a good thing. There are many times in our lives when we have been able to rescue a bad decision and make the best of it into a good solution. I believe turning "lemons into lemonade" is a critical problem-solving skill to have in life. It produces good solutions. I want to ask this: is there a difference between a good solution and the best solution? The leaders came up with a good plan, but how much better could things have worked if they had followed the Lord's plan and were not deceived in the first place? How much better could it have worked out if it were God's plan? There are people who have a good marriage without God. Imagine what it would be like with God. There are singles that have a good life without God, but what kind of life could you have with God and the Holy Spirit in your life? You have a good business without God, but what would happen if you inquired of the Lord? You have good solutions when you consult your own wisdom and experience, but what would your life be like if you consulted God's wisdom and experience?

Sometimes the enemy desires for you to live below the level of God's best. Not always does the devil give you what is evil. Sometimes the enemy gives you less than God's best. So we have good solutions, but we live beneath God's best. I want God's best for my life. I do not want just a good marriage; I want the best marriage. I do not just want a good job; I want the best job. I do not want just a good life; I want the best life. I had better inquire of the Lord. I had better ask God about it. I had better consult the Holy Spirit, my comforter, counselor, instructor, guide, and advocate. I will inquire of the Lord. The songwriter said:

What a friend we have in Jesus.
All our sins and griefs to bear;
What a privilege to carry everything to God in prayer.

THE BACKSTORY

On May 16, 1999, I stood before the congregation of the Mississippi Boulevard Christian Church of Memphis, Tennessee, and preached this very sermon, "Inquire of the Lord." I was the recommended candidate to become the senior pastor of the church. This sermon was the opportunity for the entire church to hear me preach and to consider the leaderships' recommendation of my candidacy. The next day the church would cast their vote in the affirmative or negative. My message that day was obvious: I was asking the congregation had they inquired about the Lord concerning me. They were "sampling my provisions," my résumé, credentials, references, experience, and background, but had anyone asked God about this major decision. Had anybody inquired of the Lord?

It is interesting that the stance of the sermon is had *they* inquired of the Lord and there is no reference to *my* inquiring of the Lord. I never said in the sermon that I had inquired of the Lord as to whether or not to become the pastor of Mississippi Boulevard Christian Church. I had in fact inquired of the Lord, but in reflecting thirteen years later upon my inquiry in 1999, I was tired, exhausted, and worn out in my spirit when I discerned God's will.

When I became the pastor of New Faith Baptist Church in 1982, they had just come out of a church split. The membership was down to fifty-seven people, and they were in rented facilities. My mother was a member of the church, and after the pastor resigned, they needed a preacher for Mother's Day. Knowing my mother had a son in seminary, they asked her to secure me to preach for Mother's Day. I came and preached, and then they asked me to preach the next week, as they did not have anyone that week either. I did not think any more about the church until I heard from them in September. They asked me to be the interim pastor for three months until they found a pastor.

During my interim tenure, I preached regularly, though my main job was to lead worship and provide continuity until they secured a pastor. The church started to grow. Some of the members went to the search committee and said that if the church was growing with me as the interim, didn't it make sense that it would grow with me as the pastor? The search committee agreed and, after several interviews, they asked me to become their pastor. I inquired of the Lord and my wife and I believed that the Lord was calling us to lead the New Faith Baptist Church.

Fast forward eighteen years later. We had twenty-seven acres of land, multiple buildings, a membership of four thousand, and a multimillion dollar budget. The Lord had blessed mightily, allowing us three weekend worship services and the church growing by leaps and bounds. Underneath all of the growth and progress was a deep exhaustion and weariness in my spirit that I did not recognize nor know how to deal with.

When we dedicated our first building, one of my mentors, Vincent Harding, came to celebrate with us and deliver the morning sermon. He asked me after the service, "What kind of energy does it take to build an institution?" I did not understand his question until much later. I came to believe that he meant: What kind of energy, from one's mind, body, and soul, does it take to grow a ministry to the size of New Faith, and then not only maintain at that level, but also to push it to go higher? I had no awareness of what he was asking me at the time and did not know how to respond, but I did think deeply about the question.

As we became more and more successful, I could hardly celebrate the meeting of one challenge before I took on another. Early in my first months of ministry at New Faith, I declared that we would secure land in what I know now was some overly optimistic timeframe. At that point, we were putting the building fund money in a huge plastic water jug and taking it home and bringing it back each Sunday. Well, the Lord blessed us and we got the land in that timeframe. Then the challenge was to build something on the land. I set out to meet that challenge. When we met that challenge and built our first building, then we had to fill the building and meet the increased mortgage and expenses. We filled the building, and then we needed multiple services to handle the crowd. And once we needed multiple services, we needed more staff and volunteers to handle the multiple worship services and the increased demand for services of a growing membership. And eventually we needed to add on more space to handle the operation, which meant more construction and new funds needing to be raised. The challenges went on and on.

One of the realities in most churches is that there are not extended periods of rest. In the military, if you are on the front line, they furlough you to get some rest. In the church, there is no back. There is only the next challenge. The senior pastor is always at the point leading the next challenge. I needed a sabbatical; I needed an extended time off for renewal, but there was no rest. I needed to inquire of the Lord. I could not see to request extended time and the church leadership could not see to give it to me. We were caught up in the cycle of growth and meeting the challenges we set before ourselves.

I remember that my mother begged me not to add an additional third weekend worship service. We were considering adding a Saturday night worship service that would be the third for the weekend to accommodate the crowd. She told me that I would lose my family life because I would be in service for the entire weekend. She said that it would be detrimental to my family life. She was right. For seven years, I was in three weekend worship services. I had vacations. I took a month, and sometimes two in the summer, but it was not enough. When I stood in 1999 to preach the sermon as a candidate for MBCC, I had been in three weekend worship services for seven years. I underestimated the kind of energy, from one's mind, body, and soul, it takes to grow a ministry to the size of New Faith, and then not only maintain at that level, but also to push it to go higher. By year twelve as senior pastor of New Faith, I needed a year off to rest and heal. I knew it in my soul, but I did not know how to deal with it.

When the congregation of MBCC approached me, I was eighteen years into the ministry of New Faith and weary, worn, and exhausted in my spirit. This is the message I want to deliver to the reader: You cannot inquire of the Lord and hear clearly from God when you are weary and exhausted. Make no major decisions while weary and exhausted. I am not second-guessing the decision to come to Memphis. The Lord has blessed richly and many things happened for me in Memphis that were my heart's desire. What I am suggesting is that to fully inquire of the Lord, we must get away for a while and get some rest. Get some rest! Take a vacation. Get a sabbatical! There is all kind of help for clergy who need renewal.

Ask for help, seek out help, and be honest with yourself. There were resources that I did not access.[29]

I learned this valuable lesson of not making a decision without rest from my 1999 transition to Memphis. This time, as I contemplated my transition from the pastoral role, I was rested when I inquired of the Lord. This time I made a decision with God and do not anticipate that I will suffer buyer's remorse. This time I am at peace because I inquired of the Lord. This decision is God's best for my life.

---

29. One great source of renewal for those in pastoral leadership is the Lilly Endowment Clergy Renewal Program. Check out http://www.clergyrenewal.org.

14

IF THE LORD IS PLEASED

If the LORD is pleased with us, the LORD will lead us into . . . a land flowing with milk and honey. —NUMBERS 14:8 NIV

In September 2002, on a typically southern fall Monday afternoon, I received an emergency phone call informing me that a group of fourteen church members had filed a lawsuit against me as the pastor and the church leadership. It had been threatened, several times, but not in my wildest dreams did I think that it would become a reality. I immediately went into shock, and was even more dismayed when I found the lawsuit and myself on the cover of the newspaper the next morning. My phone, as the kids say, started "blowing up." Not only did television stations start calling for interviews, folks from everywhere began to call the church, my house, my cell phone, and my wife. Based upon the instant speed of communication, the negative publicity and gossip intensified. Because I was basically in shock, I was not embarrassed. I barely held myself together as I received outpourings of encouragement from church members, family, friends, and compassionate preachers.

Several days later, the embarrassment hit, and the depths of unrelenting shame. I was supposed to be a skilled pastor. This happens to people when they start out in ministry, but not to someone who has eighteen years of experience, and successful experience at that. I remember my first preaching opportunity one week after the lawsuit. I turned the corner coming to the church and they had my name on the side of the building. When I saw my name, I broke into tears because I was embarrassed and ashamed. I was in the pastor's study, and I thought that no one would come to hear me preach. When I stepped out and the place was full, I was appreciative. You begin to hallucinate and you think that everyone knows the news. Even when people do not know, or do not care, or do not believe what they hear, the enemy convinces you that everyone knows and everyone believes it. Aside from discerning practical strategies of how to deal with this kind of massive public and open conflict in the church, the most difficult part was the feeling of embarrassment and shame. I was embarrassed and ashamed.

We all live in fear of image. Not everyone has kids, but we are afraid that our daughters will come up pregnant, our sons will end up on drugs, our brothers will drown themselves in alcohol, and our sisters will show up on crack or crystal meth. We do not tell anyone that our uncle is in prison or our aunt is suffering with mental illness. We are scared to tell people the truth about the realities that suggest our families or our ministries are not perfect. We are afraid to be honest about the conflict in our churches; the fact that conflict is there, is escalating, can erupt at any moment, and that we do not quite know what to do. We are scared of the grapevine and what people are going to say, afraid of the preachers and what the preachers are going to say. We keep up a desperate façade.

What if we worried less about our image, and were more concerned if God was pleased? Maybe we could be delivered from the opinion of people if we took seriously the promise of the text in Numbers 14:8—if the Lord is pleased with us, the Lord will lead us into a land flowing with milk and honey.

The Hebrew people had come out of slavery in Egypt and were out in the wilderness. Moses and Aaron sent twelve spies out to scout the Promised Land. When the spies returned, they gave their report to Moses and Aaron and all the people. The collective group of the spies could not agree on one report, so they submitted a majority and minority report. The majority report said that the people in the land were like giants and the Israelites were like grasshoppers, therefore, "We cannot go up and possess the land." The minority report given by Joshua and Caleb said, "The Lord our God is able and we should go up and possess the land." The people believed the majority report and massive fear and anxiety swept the camp.

The people raised their voices in 14:1, wept aloud all night, and grumbled against Moses and Aaron: "We should have died in Egypt rather than out here in this barren land. Why did the Lord bring us to this land to let us fall by the sword?" In verse 4, they even suggested, "We should choose a new leader and go back to Egypt." Based upon their massive fear and anxiety, the people panicked and were beyond rational thought.

In verse 5, Moses and Aaron fall face down in front of the whole people. Joshua and Caleb tear their clothes. Moses and Aaron plead with the people not to rebel against God and fear the people in the land. In verse 8, Joshua and Caleb say: "If the Lord is pleased with us, we will possess the land." Joshua and Caleb encouraged the people to have faith in God because, if the Lord was pleased, then the people would possess the land. Joshua and Caleb were suggesting that the ultimate factor of victory was not money, intelligence, experience, management skills, etc.; the critical factor was whether the Lord was pleased with them as a people.

In verse 10, the people responded to Joshua, Caleb, and Moses' plea with more verbal attacks. They wanted to stone the leaders. As they were screaming, God got involved. I tell leaders that, based upon my own experience, I do not care what happens, if God is pleased with you, they are not going to get you. They will howl, threaten, yell, and scream, but if God is pleased with you, then God will show up. In the middle of the people's rage, God arises. The glory of the Lord shows up at the Tent of Meeting. God interrupts the violent plans of the people and calls for a meeting with Moses

In verses 11–12, God speaks to Moses, and God is angry. God says, "How long will these people treat me with contempt? How long will they refuse to believe in me, in spite of all the miraculous signs I have performed on their behalf?" God determines that God will destroy them and start all over with Moses. God will make Moses a great nation.

In verse 13, Moses pleads with God the way that he, Joshua, and Caleb pleaded with the people. Moses is pleading with God on their behalf and the people are still screaming, "Stone them!" Moses is begging God for the people's lives, when they have whined, complained, and despised Moses and his leadership. He basically says to God, "Don't do this! The Egyptians will hear about it. They will get the report that you destroyed them (Israel). They know that you brought them out. They know that you go before them in a cloud by day and a pillar of fire by night. If you kill the Israelites, the Egyptians will say that you were not able to do what you said and so you slaughtered them in the desert. What's more, God, you are slow to anger, abounding in love and forgiving sin and rebellion. Yet you do not leave the guilty unpunished and you punish to the third and fourth generation. In accordance with your great love, forgive the sin of these people."

And because God is pleased with Moses, in verse 20, God relents. God forgives the people. But even though God forgives, God does not release them from judgment. Not one of them will make it to the Promised Land. They must wander in the wilderness until a generation dies off. Joshua and Caleb are the only ones that will walk into the Promised Land.

I am impressed with Pastor Moses. He loves God and the people. He pleads for the people to God even when the people want to kill him. How does Moses plead for them and they have just wanted to stone him? You cannot help anybody if you are not delivered from the opinion of people. If a leader is trying to please the people and the leader thinks to him or herself, "They act like this, after all I did for them," the leader is in a world of trouble. The leader will get angry and operate out of resentment and hurt feelings. And once a leader operates from hurt feelings, it becomes easy to hurt the people whom the leader leads. God will come up with a plan to destroy the people, and the leader will not plead their case. The leader will take it personally and the people will not have a shepherd. And in the leader's pain, God will say, "I am going to destroy them," and the leader will have a list of the people the leader wants to save and the rest can be destroyed. The people will have no advocate, no intercessor, and no pastor. The leader, in his/her pain, will reach out in unspiritual ways to crush the opposition, and the Lord will not be pleased. And how will God give us the victory if the Lord is not pleased with us?

Edwin H. Friedman taught that the leader's response either heightens or lowers the anxiety, panic, and rage of people. I have found that responsibility for my own behavior and actions gives me power in the most desperate situations. If I act in accordance with the mandates of Scripture, and God is pleased with my actions, then God will deliver. Moses did not attack the people back. Moses, at least in this text, did not complain about them. Moses went to God in prayer and pleaded with God on behalf of the people and pleaded with the people on behalf of God. Moses did not get anxious and maintained enough objective distance not to take the attacks personally, and yet was close enough to the people and cared enough about them to plead their case before God. The people had an advocate, intercessor, and a pastor.

Throughout the lawsuit ordeal, I conducted myself in a manner that God would be pleased about. I was a pastor for the people and pleaded the people's case to God, even though some of them were screaming, "stone him." I want to articulate several of the tangible and applicable spiritual lessons I learned that helped me not only to survive the conflict and public attack, but to overcome it, grow from it, and ultimately thank God for it. All the lessons start with the fact that my desire was for the Lord to be pleased with my and our behavior in response to the court ordeal.

I remembered Jesus. God got a hold of me as I meditated on Hebrews 12:2: "Let us fix our eyes on Jesus, the author and the finisher of our faith, who for the joy set before him endured the cross and despised the shame." The text says that he despised the shame. The cross is embarrassing. It is a place for criminals; the cross was shameful; he was a public spectacle; he was despised and rejected. The cross is embarrassing, but I noticed that he despised the shame.

In the deepest and darkest moment of the public attack, God gave me this word, which was a lifeline to a drowning preacher. God said about Jesus in this text: he was not embarrassed by the embarrassment. Without question, it is embarrassing to go through public attacks, but we have to choose to be embarrassed. It is embarrassing, but we can choose not to be embarrassed. Being embarrassed is my choice and my decision. I despised the shame. Jesus was not embarrassed by the embarrassment and neither was I. God was pleased with Jesus and I thought God would be pleased with me. I was not embarrassed and therefore did not go into hiding or other shame-faced behavior. I held my head up and carried out my responsibilities as pastor. I believe the Lord was pleased.

No matter how personal an attack may appear to be, the leader cannot take it personally. Public attacks are not personal. It is impossible to keep public attacks from happening in leadership positions. Do not take attacks personally, even if the attack is personal on the part of the perpetrator(s). After several years of relationship, I said to a young lady who had been molested by a family member that it was not personal. It was not about her or what she had on or how she looked. This violent act was about the family and how the family organized itself and allowed a lack of security and protection for girls in the family. It had to do with the man that perpetrated the act and the family more than it had to do with her. I asked her to not take the most personal act, sexual molestation, personally. Nothing was wrong with her. Something was wrong with the family.

Conflict in the church is the exact same. Often conflict is a family issue and is a result of the way that the family has organized itself to provide or not provide a place of safety and security for effective leadership. God is pleased with the one who does not take the attacks personally. God is pleased with the leader who pleads with God for the people and then pleads with the people for God. To plead with God for the people, the leader cannot take the attacks personally. It was hard, but I did not take the attacks personally and I believe the Lord was pleased.

There are no victims; there are only volunteers. There are the exceptions to this rule, such as violent crime, war crimes, natural disasters, and especially children who are victims of sexual abuse. But when I looked closely at my situation, it helped me to realize that I was not a victim. I volunteered for leadership and could handle whatever came as a result of my attempt to lead. I made a choice to lead. I was not a victim because I volunteered for the assignment. I am not a victim of my circumstances. I volunteered for my leadership assignment. I am not a victim of personal attacks; as a part of my service to God, I chose to be a leader. God is pleased when we take personal responsibility and do not blame. I am not a victim. I volunteered for this difficult assignment.

Realizing that I volunteered put me back in the position of taking responsibility for my choice. And we have consistently taught throughout these pages that whenever we acknowledge that we choose something, it is an act of empowerment. Choice is an empowering act of agency where we shape our own future and destiny. The legal troubles that I was involved in were part of the future and destiny that I chose, and it would work out for my good. I believe the Lord was pleased when I acknowledged that I was not a victim, but I volunteered for the assignment.

Vindication takes time. People can tear down in five minutes what it takes years to a lifetime to build. It is easy for people to throw mud on you, disparage your reputation, and in the words of the old Negro spiritual, "scandalize my name." I learned that sometimes it takes years to clean off the mud that people can throw on you in ten seconds. I had to learn to wait and depend on God. God will vindicate, but it takes time and you just have to wait. God is pleased when we can wait and trust God to vindicate. In the words of an old preacher, "You cannot hurry God; you just have to wait." My vindication took several years, but I was completely and absolutely vindicated. I could not rush my vindication. I had to sit in the midst of the valley and wait until God moved. I believe that God was pleased that I could wait.

Do not fight battles with unspiritual weapons. The Bible says in 2 Corinthians 10:3–4 that we do not fight with weapons that are carnal. We do not wage war as the world does. Now, I am not in any way implying that we should be passive and not fight public attacks. I am not suggesting that we simply cave in and let matters run their course. I am suggesting that we fight, but we fight with spiritual weapons and not with carnal ones. Utilizing unspiritual weapons leaves God out of the mix.

During the trial, I borrowed a phrase from Gandhi that summed up my understanding of spiritual weapons: unarmed truth. Truth is not a weapon to harm. Truth is not armed or armored, but truth is unarmed. I define unarmed truth as honesty with no pretense; truth with no excuses; no faking, no bravado, no pretense, and no blame. Truth stands by itself and has no hard or sharp projections such as spines, prickles, spurs, claws, etc. Truth is not in a state in which it may be detonated. Martin Luther King Jr. said, "A lie cannot live forever and truth crushed to the earth will rise again."[30] Truth will win. God will be pleased with my battle plan, if I base it on truth.

I needed for it to happen. Ultimately, we were victorious and the lawsuit was sent back to be resolved as a matter in our local congregation. The church exclusively had the right to address the issue and the appellate court ruled that the lower court had no "subject jurisdiction." The lower court had no business taking the case in the first place. The church addressed the issues with those members and we moved on to do the ministry that God had given our hands and hearts to do.

But after time and honest reflection over the whole experience, I came to this conclusion: I needed what happened to me. I needed to be sued. I needed to have my face plastered on the front on the newspapers. I needed to be an item on the television at 5 PM, 6 PM, and 10 PM on three stations. I needed the pain, hurt, disappointment, and doubt. I needed it to learn that the most important thing in life is if the Lord is pleased. Up to that point, I had been a deep people-pleaser, and I really tried hard to please people. I discovered in my soul, in the indescribable pain and loneliness of those hours, that one thing mattered in life: whether the Lord was pleased.

I am not posturing myself as a hero. I am just a person who grew up in a family that had issues and problems that we could not handle, and I learned some things that were not true and I lived them for a long time. But God helped me and delivered me. God delivered me from the opinion of people. I have some deliverance to go, but I thank God that, though I am not where I want to be, I am not where I used to be. I thank God for the experience of conflict and public attack. I would not wish it on anyone. I would not want my worst enemy to go through all that I went through, but I thank God for it because I am stronger and better. It took all of this for me to learn that you cannot please people. It took all this for me to learn that, if God is pleased, then I do not have to worry about pleasing people. *If the Lord is pleased with us, the Lord will lead us into a land flowing with milk and honey.*

---

30. "How Long, Not Long," speech given March 25, 1965, on the steps of the statehouse in Montgomery, Alabama, following the march from Selma.

THE BACK STORY

In the backstory to the sermon "As One with Authority," I gave the coach my response to her questions, what did I know to be true at my inner core and what did I want, really? You will remember that I said: I know God sent Jesus Christ to be the Savior of the world, and what I want, really, is to please God, proclaim the good news of Jesus Christ, and do the right thing in all relationships. This sermon returns to the core value that shapes the direction and intention of my ministry and life: I have such an intense desire to please God that I do the right thing in all relationships. This has been the belief that has guided and sustained me across thirty-one years of pastoral ministry. When people ask me how I have lasted so long, I respond that it has always been first and uppermost in my mind to please God, and if you please God, there is no way that you can be defeated. It does not mean that you will not have heartache, disappointment, battles, and stressful times. It means that you will not be overcome.

I realize that this belief is based on a tremendous amount of idealism. Idealism has been, for better or for worse, a large part of my life and leadership approach and strategy. For example, in the lawsuit and public attack, there were important choices about how to approach the situation. One choice would be the Machiavellian approach that we talked about earlier in "No Hurt Like a Church Hurt." You will remember that Machiavelli set forth clear tactics to win political battles, summarized in the statement "the end justifies the means." Even morality can be suspended to reach your goal because the end justifies the means. Winning the lawsuit was the goal and whatever one had to do to win was fair game, even if one had to annihilate the opposition.

The other side of the tactic table can be summarized in this phrase: "the means justify the ends." In other words, the means you choose to get to the end mediate the end you achieve. It is difficult to use the means of hate to achieve the ends of love. It is difficult to use the means of violence to achieve the ends of peace. It is difficult to use unspiritual means to achieve spiritual ends. The question was: How does one win the lawsuit and still please God? How does one win a decisive victory, but still leave the possibility of reconciliation after everything is done? I decided on the strategy of nonviolence and unarmed truth to please God. I idealistically determined to win the lawsuit *and* reclaim those who filed the suit. It proved not to be possible, but I carefully chose the means to accomplish this end.

Each leader must choose which approach is necessary to resolve conflict. Though I have chosen idealism, if not tempered with a heavy dose of realism, then it can look like appeasement. Appeasement makes a leader appear weak, and the opposition is emboldened to even more outrageous behavior. If the leader is overly idealistic and wants reconciliation at all costs, then the opposition will push the carrot of reconciliation out farther and farther, and behave more and more recklessly. One has only to think of the Nazi regime to have an example of appeasement that led to the furthering of the nihilistic aims of Hitler. Hitler was finally stopped with a heavy dose of military realism by several countries, including the United States. It takes a great deal of maturity to find the balance between idealism and realism. I have not always risen to the level to achieve that balance.

I want to share with the reader the greatest benefit I have experienced from the idealistic approach in my ministerial life. The chief benefit of my approach has been that I have been able to gain the trust of the majority of the people. When people see a close relationship between what a leader preaches and what a leader lives, the majority of the people trust the leader. Most people trust biblical values such as peace, justice, mercy, truth, love, reconciliation, etc., and when the people see the leader operate from biblical values, the majority of the people trust the leader. I want to emphasize, not all of the people, but many of the people. Many goals, projects, objectives, and aspirations are possible when the majority of the people trust the leader.

I have been able to be successful in ministry these thirty-one years because I adhered as closely as possible to biblical values and never lost the basic trust of the majority of any group that I pastored. Money was never missing and always properly accounted for. I never carried on illicit relationships that caused my wife, family, and the church any embarrassment or harm. I gave a hard day's work for a hard day's pay. I made every attempt to treat people fairly and to be truthful, even in the most difficult and painful situations. I believe character and integrity are the firm foundation of success in ministry. I believe that integrity, doing the right thing, and pleasing God will win in the end.

I am not suggesting that I did not make plenty of mistakes. I am not suggesting that there were not times when I was wrong, arrogant, uncaring, unspiritual, angry, and bitter. I have been appeasingly naïve and did not engage some power battles that needed to be fought. My attempt to please God has been vastly imperfect at best. But I can say this to a young preacher, pastor, or young person: do the right thing in all relationships because you have such an intense desire to please God, and you will win in the end. You will not be overcome.

I leave you with the words Julian of Norwich (c. 1342–1416), the great English mystic, who says in *The Revelation of Divine Love,* "We are given comfort in these matters of all tribulation. Because he said not, 'Thou shalt not be troubled. Thou shalt not be travailed. Thou shalt not be distressed.' He said, 'Thou shalt not be overcome.'"

You will not be overcome if the Lord is pleased.

◆ I 5 ◆

THE FACE OF GOD

So Jacob was left alone, and a man wrestled with him till day-
break. When the man saw that he could not overpower him, he
touched the socket of Jacob's hip so that his hip was wrenched
as he wrestled with the man. Then the man said, "Let me go, for
it is daybreak." But Jacob replied, "I will not let you go unless you
bless me." The man asked him, "What is your name?" "Jacob,"
he answered. Then the man said, "Your name will no longer be
Jacob, but Israel, because you have struggled with God and with
humans and have overcome." Jacob said, "Please tell me your
name." But he replied, "Why do you ask my name?" Then he
blessed him there. So Jacob called the place Peniel, saying, "It is
because I saw God face to face, and yet my life was spared."

—GENESIS 32:24–30 NIV

In many times and places in my life as a Christian, I have heard people say that they want and need to get in the face of God. I have said it myself, "I'm going home to get in God's face, or I need to get away for a minute and get in God's face." Usually, this is a declaration of an intense desire and thirst for the presence of God, and often it is assumed that in the presence of God there will be sweetness, joy, peace, and clarity.

And, in fact, ultimately there is in the presence of God sweetness, joy, peace, and clarity. But what we do not often acknowledge is that we come to sweetness, joy, peace, and clarity by a process of struggle, most often a huge, awesome, and almost overwhelming struggle just like Jacob experienced. Jacob wrestled with God and prevailed, and when Jacob finished, he called the place Peniel, meaning "God's face," or, I have seen the face of God and survived. Have you ever been to God's face?

I am working on what Joan Chittister, in her book *Scarred by Struggle, Transformed by Hope* calls a "spirituality of struggle." She argues that a spirituality of struggle moves beyond the spiritual life as a matter of simply doing good works, earning a good reputation, practicing social virtues, or being regular in church attendance and participation. If we are not careful, she argues, from these practices we develop easy and cheap answers to life. With our cheap religion and surface spirituality, we tie life into a nice and easy bow. We develop our church clichés and pat spiritual responses like "When praises go up, blessings come down," "God is good," and somebody screams back, "All the time." But while we are quoting our clichés something happens. Chittister says that there comes "a blow . . . so momentous, so sudden, so unexpected, and so unwanted that there is no way whatsoever to prepare for its coming." It comes out of nowhere and it makes our heart tremble and our knees buckle. Chittister continues, "The struggle that threatens to take us down into the pit of life is whatever we cannot imagine living without— money or status, love or acceptance or public approval or things."[31] We find ourselves wrestling in the middle of the night with unnamed forces, powers beyond our ability to control and our ability to know. The easy answers and the clichés do not work. And all of a sudden, you realize that you are just like Jacob wrestling in a life and death struggle in the middle of the night.

You remember Jacob: he was the son of Isaac and Rebecca, the grandson of Abraham and Sarah, and the twin brother of Esau. You remember Jacob: he was married to Rachel and Leah and had twelve sons and several daughters. You remember Jacob: his name means trickster (heel,

---

31. Chittister, *Scarred by Struggle*, 89.

leg-puller). He tricked his brother out of his birthright; he tricked his father for his brother's blessing. As a result, his brother Esau was angry with him and hated him for his trickery. His mother sent him to Uncle Laban's to let the heat die down.

Jacob left Beersheba and set out to Uncle Laban in Haran. It was a long journey and he found a place to sleep at night because the sun had set. He took one of the stones and used it as a pillow. He dreamed that there was a stairway set on the ground and its top reached heaven; there were angels going up and coming down. And at the top of the ladder he saw God and God said to him that he would receive the land on which he was sleeping and God would make his descendants like the dust of the earth in the north, south, east, and west, and all the families of the earth would be blessed in his family. God said, "I will protect you and not leave you. I will be with you. I will bring you back to this land. I will not leave you until I have done all that I have told you." Jacob named the place "Bethel," saying, "Surely this is the house of God." Jacob vowed a vow that night saying that if God stands by me and protects me on this journey, keeps me with food and clothing, brings me back in one piece to my father's house, then this God will be my God.

Jacob continued the journey to Uncle Laban's house. Ultimately, after being tricked and misused by his Uncle Laban in the matter of Rachel and Leah, and working extended years for his uncle, he tricked and misused Uncle Laban. Uncle Laban pursued Jacob, and because the Lord spoke to Laban not to harm Jacob, they reconciled and Jacob departed and crossed over into Canaan to return to his father. On his way, the text says that angels met him.

Jacob sent word to his brother Esau that he wanted to reconcile. The report came back that Esau was headed his way with four hundred men and Jacob was fearful for his life and his family. He sent peace offerings to Esau in waves, hoping to placate him: two hundred female goats, twenty male goats, two hundred sheep and twenty rams, thirty camels with their nursing young, forty cows, ten bulls, twenty female donkeys, and ten male donkeys. He put a male servant in front of each herd and told them to keep a healthy space between them. He instructed them: when Esau comes close and says, "Who owns these?" they were to say,

"Your servant Jacob. They are a gift to my master Esau." The easy answers were not working anymore. Jacob was worried, scared, and afraid. He attempted to placate and patronize his brother.

That same night, worried and afraid, he arose. He sent his two wives and two maidservants and his eleven children across the river. Along with the family, he sent everything that he owned, cattle and all his possessions. But Jacob stayed back alone, fearful, anxious, scared for his life and desperate because of his past. All of a sudden, he was ambushed, attacked, waylaid, trapped, ensnared, assaulted; something came out of nowhere, so sudden, so momentous, so overwhelming, so unwanted, and so surprising. His first thought: Is this Esau? No! He is wrestling with a foe that is much more powerful than he or Esau, a foe made all the more powerful by the fact that the attack is an ambush at night, meant to catch Jacob unaware and with the elements of darkness and surprise to overcome him quickly, subdue him, and make a hasty exit. The struggle threatens to take him down into the pit of life, where he is forced to live without whatever he cannot imagine living without, money, status, love, family, acceptance, public approval, or material things. This is a life and death struggle for his sanity, his identity, his hope, for his very soul. Ever been there? Have you ever been to God's face?

Can I make the life and death struggle plain for you? A young woman sits with lines of cocaine trying to decide whether or not to take a hit. To take a hit now is to lose everything. She knows it will result in a weekend binge and her husband will leave and take the children and abandon her because she has broken so many promises before. If she does it, she feels better temporarily, but if she does it she loses everything. And so she sits wrestling like Jacob with unseen forces more powerful than she, wrestling like Jacob for her sanity, her identity, her hope, and her very soul. Have you ever been there? Have you ever been to God's face?

A young preacher sits with a gun. He has broken the marriage vows once again. It has been discovered and is public now. It is in the newspapers and on television; the scandal is of epic proportions. He fears he will lose everything now. He looks at the gun and he looks at the Bible, looks at the gun and looks at the Bible, struggling for his sanity, struggling for his hope, and ultimately struggling for his life, wrestling like Jacob with unseen forces more powerful than he. Have you even been there? Wrestling for your sanity, your soul, and your life? Have you ever been to God's face?

The text says that Jacob wrestled all night. He encountered a more powerful opponent with the element of surprise, but Jacob wrestled all night. He did not quit, did not give up, did not give out and give in. He was a trickster, a leg-puller, and a heel, but his trickster ways would not give him the power to last all night. For the first time in his life, he had to deal straight up. No tricks, no manipulations, no stealing birthrights and blessings, no games, no manipulating help from mother, no cheap answers, no surface spirituality, no clichés—sometimes you have to deal straight up. The pain, doubt, and uncertainty is real, and you cannot escape it. You have to deal with it and wrestle with it. He is struggling for his life, for his sanity, and for his hope.

Sometimes you have to tell the truth. Sometimes you have to 'fess up, own up, take responsibility, and tell the truth. Sometimes you cannot go around it or over it or under it; sometimes you have to go straight through the middle of a thing. Sometimes truth is my only hope, to tell the truth is my only hope. He deals straight up and says: I have been a trickster, a heel, a leg-puller, but back there sleeping on that ground God gave me a promise. When I saw the ladder into heaven, God said: "I will give you the ground on which you are sleeping to you and your descendants. I will protect you and not leave you; I will be with you, and I will bring you back to this land and I will not leave you until I have done all that I have told you. Your descendants will be like the dust of the earth." He tells the truth about himself: he is a trickster, a heel, and a leg-puller—but a trickster, a heel, and a leg-puller with a promise. He holds on to the promise and it gives him the power to struggle all night.

When it is a real struggle like this, there is not always a clear winner. He is grappling with an opponent that is stronger than he is and sometimes it is enough to prevail, to last to the very last, to be in the fight to the end, to keep up, to keep on, to carry on, to persist, to endure, and to survive. Sometimes it is enough to say, as did the songwriter, "I'm still here. I've made it through, so have you. I've come through the fire, I've come through the flood; I'm still here."[32]

Our society is into winners and losers. We think that we have to win everything. But in this text there is no clear sign that Jacob won; he prevailed, he lasted. Sometimes victory is to prevail, to last, to make it to the pulpit to preach for one more week, to make the bill payment one more month, to get to church for one more Sunday, to get the kids off to school for one more day. Sometimes it is victory to make it one more day and say, I'm still here.

Now do not miss this: they are in mortal combat. They are tussling on the ground and Jacob is fighting for his life. One of my preaching students made this point in talking about this text: Jacob and his opponent were in a wrestling match and the opponent picked up Jacob and body slammed him to the ground like we see in the professional wrestling matches on television. And when Jacob's body came crashing to the earth, it knocked the breath completely out of him. But from the ground, he could see the stars. When he saw the stars, he remembered the ladders and the angels going up and down and that God gave him a promise. He finds the strength to wrestle for another round because of the promise. The opponent picks him up again. This time the opponent slams him face down and when his face hits the ground the dust of the earth gets in his mouth and his nostrils. As he is eating dirt, he remembers that God said his descendants would be like the dust of the earth. He remembers the promise and finds strength to wrestle for one more round. Have you ever been there? Ever been to God's face?

The text says, "The one that Jacob wrestled with saw that he could not prevail so he struck his hip and threw his hip out of joint." Sometimes the enemy sees that he cannot defeat you, so he wounds you in the hope that you will quit because you are wounded. You will give up because you are wounded. You will stop because you are wounded. But look at this: Jacob is wounded, but he is still wrestling. He is hurt, but he is still in the game. In this wrestling, you will pick up some wounds and you will pick

---

32. Albertina Walker, "I'm Still Here," http://www.lyriczz.com/lyrics/albertina-walker/53436-i'm-still-here/, accessed 12/1/12.

up some scars. In Peniel, that is, God's face, you will get a limp. You will get your feelings hurt. You will be disappointed. You will be betrayed. But even though his hip is out of socket, Jacob is still wrestling. He is still tussling, and even after making him limp his opponent says, "Let me go, for day is breaking." He is wounded but his opponent asks to be let go.

Jacob says to him, "You cannot leave until you bless me." The word "bless" literally means "a transfer of strength." When you bless someone you transfer to them your strength. I am in this struggle and this struggle can transfer me its strength. You cannot leave until you transfer me some of your strength. Devil, you sent this to kill me, but transfer me your strength in the attack. God will make your enemies bless you and transfer you their strength.

The man asks Jacob his name. And he said, "Jacob." The man, in turn, says "You shall no longer be called Jacob, but now Israel, for you have striven with God and with humans and have prevailed." He gets a new name, Israel. Eugene Peterson translates Israel to mean "God-wrestler." He has lasted. He is still struggling, still fighting, and still holding on. He has not won, but he is not looking for victory. He is only looking to last one more day. This is hope, hard-fought, hard-won, and real. Not cotton candy or clichés, but hope hard-fought, hard-won, and real. Jacob has received a transfer of strength, but he earned it and he got a new name. The change of Jacob's name presupposes the establishment of a nation. He was Jacob the trickster, but now he is the founder of a nation. He was a heel and a leg-puller and now he is the father of the twelve sons who will give rise to the twelve tribes. He is a man. He is the father of a nation. The promise that he saw on the ground has been fulfilled.

And Jacob called the place "God's face." Jacob has seen the face of God and has survived. God's face is the place where a traveler who had a terrifying experience of a hostile attack ended with wrestling a "blessing" from his opponent. God's face is the place where we have to deal straight up, no tricks, lies, and deceits. God's face is a place where victory is not always winning; victory is to last. God's face is where you get a limp and even though you are limping you are still on the battlefield. God face is the place where you learn to ask for a blessing, a transfer of strength. God's face is where you get a new name. God face is the place where you remember the promise, last because of the promise, and see the promised fulfilled. And he named the place Peniel, God's face, for he had seen the face of God and survived.

I've been to God's face. Have you ever been to God's face? I've been to God's face. I have been ambushed. Attacked. But from that situation I wrestled a blessing. From the chaos and the mess and the tears and the pain, I snatched a victory. I remembered the promise. God said that I would receive the land on which I was sleeping and God would make my descendants like the dust of the earth in the north, south, east, and west, and all the families of the earth would be blessed in my family. God said I will protect you and not leave you and I will be with you, and I will bring you back to this land and I will not leave you until I have done all that I have told you. And this God will be my God forever and ever. This God will be my God forever and evermore. Have you ever been to God's face? If not, then you will. Your wrestling match, ambush, and name change are on the way.

THE BACKSTORY

When one concludes a ministry in a particular place, one walks slowly and methodically across memory and remembrance to consider the meaning and significance of one's time and contribution. What we usually do is consider a list of our accomplishments and, based upon that list, we conclude our legacy. I wanted something more than a list of what was accomplished because that seemed to be more focused on the outside in. I wanted to discern what my time in Memphis meant inside out. What did I learn about what I believed to be true and what I wanted, really? How did the experience at Mississippi Boulevard Christian Church lead to the development of my inner core? I was more concerned about my inner core than my outer legacy.

I was introduced to the concept of the "spirituality of struggle" by Joan Chittister in her book *Scarred by Struggle*. The chief example of the spirituality of struggle was Jacob wrestling with an adversary in Genesis 32. I read the entire biblical account of the story of Jacob. God woke me up for two weeks straight at 3:00 o'clock each morning. I would return to the exact same place in my home and read Genesis 32. Following my reading of the text, I would pray, mediate, write, and listen for God to reveal the meaning to me. I could not explain it, but this text and God were speaking to my very soul.

To gain a better sense of the exegetical meaning of the text, I read multiple versions. I read many and various commentaries and study resources, the most helpful being Claus Westerman's *Genesis 12–36* and the Jewish Torah Commentary.[33] I had an almost insatiable appetite for this text. The phrase that attracted me the most from the text was "God's face." I could not get over the fact that Jacob called the place of his life and death struggle "God's face." I even named the upstairs place in my home, my devotional place, where I read this text for two straight weeks, "God's face." I wrestled with God about this text in God's face.

It was in this two-week timeframe that I came to another level of peace with my retirement as the pastor of Mississippi Boulevard Christian Church. I experienced myself in the Genesis 32 text as a traveler who had come to Memphis and was ambushed and attacked by unseen and unnamed forces more powerful than myself. I found myself wrestling for my sanity, my hope, and my life. I was Jacob wrestling with a powerful adversary in the middle of the night.

At the onset of my ministry, I was given a promise by God that I would reach and touch people. In my struggles in Memphis, with an opponent more powerful than myself, I held on to the promise. I was a heel and a trickster who could be considered naïve and nonconfrontational, but I wrestled. I did not quit. I did not give up. Based upon the promise, I lasted the night. How can you be naïve and nonconfrontational and you last all night in the struggle? You can last if you focus on the promise.

For much of my ministry, I thought that victory was in winning, such as expanding the membership, building new buildings, being known as a "church growth expert," more and better speaking engagements, etc. All of this was outside in and not inside out. I learned that the victory was not in winning; victory was to prevail, to last, to wrestle on based on resources from the inside out. I learned my inner strength and inner resolve to hold on to the promise of God, even though I was wounded and struggling against a more powerful opponent. I learned that real victory was inside out and not outside in.

Because I held on to the promise and lasted, I received a transfer of strength. I received a new name. I was no longer a trickster and a heel who was naïve and nonconfrontational, but I became tenacious and unmovable. I found that I had

---

33. Claus Westermann, *Genesis 12–36: A Continental Commentary*, trans. John J. Scullion (Minneapolis: Fortress Press, 1995); Nahum M. Sarna, The Jewish Publication Society Torah Commentary, *Genesis* (Philadelphia: Jewish Publication Society, 1989).

moved beyond superficial and surface spirituality. I moved beyond clichés and living outside in. I learned the power of choice. I learned hope that was real was hard-fought and hard-won. I possessed a hope that looked at the worst and still made the choice to serve and believe. I found out that I had a soul made of titanium. I was limping from the wounds of the battle, but I had a new name. My name was inside out. I was once called senior pastor, and now, by the power of choice, I would be called professor of preaching.

I learned one final thing. You cannot leave a place healthy and whole until you bless it. Jacob blessed the place of his life and death struggle. He called it Peniel, saying it was God's face. I blessed Mississippi Boulevard Christian Church and Memphis and called it Peniel, for it was there I met God face to face, and yet my life was spared.

✦ I 6 ✦

LEAVINGS, ENDINGS, AND LETTING GO

Then Paul went down on his knees, all of them kneeling with
him, and prayed. And then a river of tears. Much clinging to
Paul, not wanting to let him go. They knew they would never see
him again—he had told them quite plainly. The pain cut deep.
Then, bravely, they walked him to the ship.

—ACTS 20:36–38 MSG

I do not do leavings and endings well. Leavings, endings, and separating from people that I love, I do not do very well. Mostly, I deny it as long as possible until I cannot deny it any further. Leavings, endings, and separations from people that I love make me sad and make me cry. I am not alone in this—leavings, endings, and separating from loved ones make a whole lot of us cry. I go through the airport often, and once I saw a mother get out of the car and follow the young son in military uniform to the ticket counter. The ticket is done; the bags are checked, and it is time for him to head through the security checkpoint. The mother grabs that boy and holds him for dear life. The tears flowed freely, unashamedly, and unapologetically. I wondered how long it would be before they would see each other again. Or maybe, because of where he was stationed, she hugged him as if she worried that it might be the last time she saw him. I do not do leavings and endings well. Leavings, endings, and letting go make me cry.

One of my best friends, my high school locker partner, and I have been friends for almost forty years. When his mother died, he did all the work to arrange the funeral. He orchestrated and took care of everything. We went to the cemetery and the pastor did the committal. We were walking away from the casket heading back to the car and he turned to me, looked me square in the face, and said with every ounce of seriousness, "I cannot leave momma out here." And in that moment, the dam broke; he collapsed in my arms and wept. I held my friend and I cried too. I do not do leavings well. Leavings, endings, and separating from someone that I love, I do not do well. Leavings, endings, and separations from people that I love make me sad and make me cry.

When I think about it, I am not sure that we know a whole lot about leavings, endings, and separating. It is called letting go. We do not know much about letting go. Someone once said that in matters of love we only need to practice letting go, for holding on comes easily, and we do not need to learn it. We already know in matters of love how to clutch, how to grab tight, how to keep close, and how to hold on. We need in love to learn how to let people go. We all hate to admit it, but there is a time for letting go. There is a time for leavings. And I hate to say it because I do not do well with leavings, endings, and separating from people that I love, but we have come to the moment for me to take my leave; for me to let you go and for you to let me go. I do not do endings and leavings well. There are many people who do not do leavings well. Leavings, endings, and separations from people that you love make you sad and make you cry. Our text in Acts 20 is about leavings, endings, separations, and letting go. Paul and the Ephesian elders could no longer deny the reality that it was time for letting go.

The backdrop to our text is that Paul does not want to be slowed down on his way to Jerusalem, for he desires to get there, if possible, by the day of Pentecost. Though Paul is facing certain imprisonment in Jerusalem, he wants to get there to celebrate the birthday of the church, the outpouring of the Holy Spirit on the church in Acts 2. Paul decides to sail past Ephesus, but his pastor's heart and love for the Ephesians has him conflicted. He decides that rather than go to Ephesus, he would stop in Miletus and summon the elders from Ephesus, some thirty-odd miles away. The elders arrive and Paul speaks to the elders openly and honestly.

First, Paul recounts his history of service (in vv. 17–21). Paul reminds them of the model life he has lived as he served the Lord. Paul's allegiance to his Lord determined the conduct of his ministry. His leadership was servant leadership, the humility of a lowly mind, for he shed the tears of a tender heart, sorrowing over rejections of the gospel outside of the church and resistance to its full work within the church. Paul mentions especially that he was severely tested by the plots of the Jews. His was the steadfast endurance of a tough skin in the face of trials. He tells them that he has gone house to house and also publicly preaching and teaching them anything he thought would be beneficial. He has declared to everyone that they must turn to God in repentance and have faith in the Lord Jesus Christ.

In vv. 22–24, Paul tells them that there is another urgency on him now. Another call has come from God, and he is compelled to go to Jerusalem. The Spirit has spoken and Paul must follow. Paul says, I am not sure what will happen when I get there; the Spirit has let me know repeatedly that there would be hard times and imprisonment. But that does not matter. What matters is to finish what the Master gave me to do: to let everyone know about the incredibly extravagant generosity of God, to let everyone know about Jesus.

In vv. 25–27, he announces that they were not going to see him again, and this is goodbye. He tells them that he has done his best. He declares that he is innocent of the blood of all men and women. He gave everything he had and held nothing back. He says he taught everything that God gave him to teach.

In vv. 28–31, he says to the elders: It is up to you now. You are in charge. You are the spiritual leaders. He then gives them several admonitions and warnings:

- Be on your toes for yourselves and the congregation of sheep;
- Guard and protect the people;
- Vicious wolves are going to rise up from among the flock and seduce people into following them rather than Jesus;

- The Holy Spirit has put you in charge of these people;
- Stay awake and guard your hearts—God thought enough of these people to die for them.

He tells them to be on guard and reminds them that for three years he never stopped warning them night and day, and with tears.

In v. 32 he says, "I am turning you over to God." He says that he is committing them to God, our marvelous God, whose gracious Word can make you into what God wants you to be and give you everything that you could possibly need in this community of holy friends. He leaves them with the Word of God that can make them into what God wants them to be and give them everything that they could ever need in this community of holy friends. I love that name for the church: a community of holy friends.

In vv. 33–35, he talks about the principle of generosity. He admits that he was never into money or fashion. He says that he worked to meet his own basic needs and the needs of those who worked with him. He recounts that he took care of the weak. In other biblical language, he fed the hungry and clothed the naked. And then he shares with them these immortal words: It is more blessed to give than to receive. His final word to them is about generosity. One commentator suggested that, as they arrived from Ephesus, the elders probably brought with them provision for Paul to help him on his journey. It was in the context of receiving and being thankful for their provision that Paul makes the comment that it is more blessed to give than to receive.

Then, we finally arrive at the focal verses of our text, vv. 36–38:

Then Paul went down on his knees, all of them kneeling with him, and prayed. And then a river of tears. Much clinging to Paul, not wanting to let him go. They knew they would never see him again—he told them quite plainly. The pain cut deep. Then, bravely, they walked him to the ship.

Paul now seals his farewell with prayer. Falling on his knees, he acts out his total submission to the Lord. The elders, in their affectionate devotion to Paul, join him in prayer. After the prayer, there is much weeping, the sound of loud and demonstrative wailing and mourning. They fall on Paul's neck and repeatedly kiss him. In ancient culture a parting kiss on the cheek, forehead, shoulder, or hand was a sign of grateful respect and love. The emotion of the parting is especially heightened by the anguish of knowing they will not see Paul again. This heightened anguish is described by the use of hyperbole: they cried a river of tears. They clung to Paul because they did not want to let him go. What anguished them the most was that they would not see him again. His leaving was one thing, but when he said they would not see him again, it tore them up. The text says the pain was very deep.

Now, this is why I do not like leavings, endings, and letting go: the pain cuts so deep. I cry a river of tears. My tendency is to cling and not let go. We know that, at the point of separation, there is much wailing and mourning. We do not want to cry like this. We do not want to hurt like this. I do not do endings, leavings, and letting go well.

But in our text something happens. Something shifts and the text says, they cried a river of tears and the pain was very deep, but *bravely, they walked him down to the ship.* Tearfully, but courageously, with hearts hurting and fighting to be strong, they submit to the will of God, and *bravely, they walked him down to the ship.*

This whole text turns on the adverb "bravely." It might be that the difference between leaving, endings, and letting go well is not the amount of tears or the clinging, or the fact that we wail and mourn, but whether we can behave bravely. We think that if we wail, mourn, and cling that we are not doing leavings, endings, and letting go well. It is not the wailing and the mourning that are bad, but as we wail and mourn, can we be brave? Maybe we do not do leavings, endings, and letting go well because we are afraid that we are not brave. I want to tell someone today that you are brave. Even though many of you do not do leavings, endings, and letting go well, you have done this ending of me as the pastor of Mississippi Boulevard Christian Church well. You are to be commended. The celebrations and the kindness that has been extended to my family have been marvelous. Some of you have broken into tears as you greeted me during the many days of this transition, and I have seen so many of you be brave. This can be said of you—bravely, they walked him down to the ship.

Bravely, you have walked me to the ship. Though you do not do endings well, you did this ending well.

Even though I do not do leavings, endings, and letting go well, I have done this leaving well. I have had my moments. There have been several times that I have been filled with fear and dread and considered rescinding my decision. I have some uncertainty about how I will feel when I am no longer your pastor. But, regardless of the pain, I kept going forward. I have been brave and I go bravely down to the ship. You and I are crying and clinging, but we *bravely* go down to the ship. You and I have fashioned a healthy model for leaving, ending, and letting go that I believe can be duplicated by many other churches.

Bravely, they walk him to the ship. Notice that they walk him. I have an image in mind of their emotional departure; they are crying and Paul is crying, but together they walk each other to the ship. It is two steps forward and one step backward, as they have fear and dread of reaching the ship. There are still tears, clinging, pain, and much gratitude. They give Paul many kind words and well-wishes. Paul gives them many kind words and well-wishes. Everyone is thankful to God, for they are at peace, despite their tears, that this is the will of God. The decision has already been made. They are able to acknowledge that they are at the point of no return. They do not know how they are doing it, but they are getting to the ship. This is leaving well. This is letting go and letting God. This is being brave.

And then Paul has to get on the ship. They watch Paul as he boards and has his ticket punched. They plant themselves on the dock to see Paul off, and Paul plants himself on the deck of the ship to watch them off. The captain unfurls the sails. The anchor is lifted. Paul is waving to them, and they are waving to Paul. The tears come fast and furious on both sides, but they still wave. And as the ship gets farther out, Paul's hand becomes smaller and their hands become smaller. And then smaller and smaller. They wave even more furiously until the ship disappears, and they can see Paul no more.

They turn to head back to Ephesus. They tell themselves that the energy cannot be spent back in the past. The energy is spent making the most effective choices for a new future. When they think about Paul, they know that the future that awaits him is opportunity. And when they walk away from the dock, what they do not fully realize yet is that opportunity awaits them also. As they look back to Ephesus, they notice a very small hand waving to them. It is almost indistinguishable, but it is a hand that is waving. As they get closer and closer, the hand gets larger and larger. They get closer and closer and the hand is bigger and bigger. It is the hand of the new pastor bidding them to come home. God has already provided. I say to you, my church family, that God has already provided.

As I leave you now, that is my final word: the Lord has already provided . . . God is Jehovah-Jireh, the one who sees beforehand and has already provided.

THE BACKSTORY

I write this on the Saturday evening before I will deliver "Leavings, Endings, and Letting Go," my final sermon at the Mississippi Boulevard Christian Church. After tomorrow, for the first time in thirty-one years, I will no longer have a dedicated Sunday morning post to preach as pastor and leader of a congregation. It feels strange to visualize that I will move into the realm of the guest preacher after facing the wonderful challenge of constructing the weekly sermon for so many years. Not that there is anything wrong with the guest preacher role, but I feel a strong sense of loss at the closure of the weekly preaching responsibility of the pastoral role. What will happen to my weekly discipline of sermon preparation? What will happen to my homiletical mind that is always looking for preaching material because of the imperative to always have a fresh word for Sunday? What if I do not have sufficient engagements to preach regularly and often? What if I lose my ability to continuously improve as a preacher for lack of opportunities? These are all thoughts that race across my mind as I realize what a privilege I have been allowed these past thirty-one years to have a pulpit to preach from every Sunday. It dawns on me that some of my grief about the loss of preaching in the pastoral role is the concept of "loss aversion."

In 1979, two Israeli psychologists, Daniel Kahneman and Amos Tversky, demonstrated the concept of "loss aversion." Kahneman and Tversky coined the phrase after giving their students a survey requesting their preferences for certain gambling bets. They noticed that when a person was offered a gamble on the toss of a coin and was told that losing would cost twenty dollars, the player demanded on average forty dollars for winning. The pain of a loss was twice as potent as the pleasure generated by a gain, or, in other words, "losing something makes you twice as miserable as gaining the same thing makes you happy."[34] Kahneman and Tversky concluded that in human decision making, losses loom larger than gains. The desire to avoid anything that smacks of a loss often shapes our behavior, leading us to exaggerate, mourn, resist, and avoid loss at all costs. It dawned on me that my lament about no longer preaching from the pastoral role was more a focus on what I was losing rather than what I was gaining in my new assignment.

The acknowledgment of loss aversion does not mean that there will not be grief. I know that there will be tears tomorrow. I know that the separation will be painful and the church and I will together cry a river of tears. But when I remember the concept of loss aversion, I decide to focus on the fact that there is excitement in having the opportunity to fully release my passion inside out. When passion meets opportunity from the inside out, it fosters a contagion of positive energy and joy in one's life. While I will not have a congregation every Sunday to preach to, I will have a tremendous opportunity to fulfill my passion, generate positive energy from the inside out, and continue to improve my preaching.

For example, I am going to read and re-read all of the best preaching books in the field of homiletics. I have been so busy practicing preaching that I have fallen behind on some of the best reading about preaching. Then, I am going to construct an audio and video library of preaching that will be a resource in my further research, writing, and practice of preaching. Next, I am going to get some rest. I have done a tremendous amount of preaching in these last thirty-one years. In some respects, I have not taken the time to renew, refresh, and restore my energy. One of the chief difficulties of being a pastor/preacher is that one is so busy feeding other people the Word of God that one often neglects the word of God for oneself. Far too many preachers only read the Bible to find sermons. I will have the opportunity to find a deeper devotional and prayer life for my own soul without the needs of a congregation uppermost in my mind. I wonder if preachers ought to sometimes take a sabbatical from preaching for the benefit of their own souls. After getting some rest, I have at least three or four more books to write.

---

34. Richard H. Thaler and Cass R. Sunstein, *Nudge: Improving Decisions about Health, Wealth, and Happiness* (New York: Penguin Books, 2009), 33.

Lastly, I will get the preaching opportunities that God sends my way, and it will be enough. God will provide the opportunities. I will have the opportunity to live my passion from the inside out.

You will remember from the introduction to this book what I told the congregation on July 2, 2012, at the announcement of my retirement:

> After much prayer, it is clear to me that in the closing years of my ministry, it is my life's work now to develop, mentor, encourage, inspire, and do whatever is necessary to cultivate a cadre of scribes and scholars, African American and otherwise, who are committed to transforming the world through sharing the genius of the African American preaching tradition.

I would also like to coach pastors and churches to help them meet their ministry needs. I am excited about my life's work now. I am excited about my new future. I will teach preaching and share the insights and learning from more than thirty-one years of preaching every Sunday, and I will coach. I will miss preaching to a local congregation each Sunday. I will miss the regular and ongoing relationship in people's lives and seeing the Word of God transform and work wonders of growth. But I know that I have made the choice, and I have made the choice from the inside out. Tomorrow, when I preach my final sermon and say goodbye, I anticipate that I will be calmer than I could have ever expected. When we speak and live inside out, we are calm.

As I board the ship, my hand is waving to Mississippi Boulevard Christian Church back on the shore. The ship leaves port, and though I wave and wave, their hands get smaller and smaller, until finally I can see them no more. With tears in my eyes, I then turn and look in the opposite direction of the shore, and I see small hands waving to greet me. They are faint and far, but as we come closer and closer, the hands get larger and larger. It is students and pastors who want to learn and improve their preaching—an entire preaching community is beckoning for me to come. It is pastors and church leaders who would like me to use my thirty-one years of learning and experience to coach them. And I know that this is the time where passion meets opportunity in my life. I am so very grateful and thankful. Thank you, Christian Theological Seminary.

Thank you to the New Faith Baptist Church International of Matteson, Illinois, and thank you to the Mississippi Boulevard Christian Church of Memphis, Tennessee. These two congregations have allowed me, for eighteen and thirteen years, respectively, to hear from the Lord and express freely and openly in the preaching moment what I have heard, and to serve as their pastor. Thank you for teaching me how to preach. Thank you for suffering some of my experimentation, and, as a friend of mine says, "allowing me the opportunity to practice preaching." So much gratitude is in my heart. I am grateful for the privilege to have served as your pastor. I turn now to embrace the hands that are waving to me as I approach the shore of my new assignment.

FRANK A. THOMAS and JOYCE SCOTT THOMAS
earned their Certified Professional Coaching Certificate (CPC)
and ELI-MP certification from the Institute for Professional
Excellence in Coaching (iPEC). Both are available to coach in
corporate, executive, business, life, personal, or group settings.

Frank A. Thomas is most passionate about coaching
pastors in the areas of leadership, wellness, and preaching,

and

Joyce S. Thomas in helping pastors' spouses find
health, celebration, and balance.

For more information, visit www.preacherscoach.com.

Visit and "like" Rev. Frank A. Thomas on
Facebook—www.facebook/the preacherscoach—
and follow him on Twitter—@drfrankathomas.

For more information about preaching resources
by Frank A. Thomas, visit www.preacherscoach.com,
www.theafricanamericanpulpit.com, and
www.preachingwithsacredfire.com.

Books by Frank A. Thomas

for more information or to purchase, go to www.preacherscoach.com

THE CHOICE
Living Your Passion Inside Out

Hope for Life International Books, 2013 / ISBN 978-0-9820169-9-2
Thomas describes the spiritual and coaching process by which he came to announce his retirement as the senior pastor of Mississippi Boulevard Christian Church after thirty-one years as a senior pastor. Follow Thomas's journey to make the choice to live his passion from the inside out, from several years of planning to his final Sunday and departure. The book will illustrate and explain how you too can live your passion inside out.

THEY LIKE TO NEVER QUIT PRAISIN' GOD
The Role of Celebration in Preaching

Cleveland: Pilgrim Press, 1997, 2013 / ISBN 978-0-8298-1978-6
This classic, critically acclaimed, and highly regarded work is seen by many as the common cure for bad preaching. The book describes the method of how to preach a celebrative sermon. Revised and updated August 2013, with two new chapters and one new sermon—a must have for every preacher, teacher, and communicator.

AMERICAN DREAM 2.0
A Christian Way Out of the Great Recession

Nashville: Abingdon, 2012 / paperback ISBN 9781426753909 /
e-book ISBN 9781426756788
There is a dark side to the American dream, too—one that we don't talk about much in polite company. Our challenge is to develop American Dream 2.0, a sustainable future free from exploitation and domination and more aligned with Jesus' vision of the kingdom of God and Martin Luther King Jr.'s vision of the "Beloved Community."

PREACHING WITH SACRED FIRE
An Anthology of African American Sermons, 1750 to the Present

New York: W.W. Norton, 2010 / ISBN 978-0-393-05831-4

www.preachingwithsacredfire.com

Preaching with Sacred Fire, co-edited with Martha Simmons, offers a rare view of the too often unheralded role of the African American preacher in American history. This anthology includes selections from Jarena Lee, Frederick Douglass, Malcolm X, Martin Luther King Jr., Gardner C. Taylor, Prathia Hall, and many others. It is a unique and powerful work that captures the stunning diversity of the cultural and historical legacy of African American preaching.

THE LORD'S PRAYER
In Times Such as These

St. Louis: Chalice Press, 2002 / ISBN 9780827221352

Originally written as a devotional reflection from the Lord's Prayer after the historic and tragic events of 9-11-01, the book is relevant to anyone going through a difficult time who wants to pray the Lord's Prayer as a source of comfort, courage, and inspiration. The Lord's Prayer has been an anchor, a refuge, and a framework for many to reach and contact God.

SPIRITUAL MATURITY
Preserving Congregational Health and Balance

Minneapolis: Fortress Press, 2002 / ISBN: 9780800630867

Spiritual Maturity offers a holistic solution-based model of spiritual maturity for creating and preserving healthy congregations. It helps lay and clergy leaders take a close look at the styles of church leadership, methods of information flow, and levels of participation that exist within the church body. This work will help improve the health of your congregational body.

WHAT'S LOVE GOT TO DO WITH IT? LOVE, POWER, SEX, AND GOD
ed. Jini Kilgrow Ross

Valley Forge: Judson Press, 2001 / ISBN 9780817013912, workbook ISBN U1433

What's Love Got to Do with It? Written to offer biblical truth and wisdom of God to those who desire healthy and whole relationships, the book grapples honestly with relationship issues—such as relationship addiction, overemphasis on sex in relationships, abuse of self to get love, etc.—in order to develop positive personal, family, and social relationships. The separate workbook is ideal for daily devotions, book clubs, or group study.

9-11-01
African American Preachers Respond to an American Tragedy

Valley Forge: Judson Press, 2001 / ISBN: 978-0817014353

African American preachers offer a variety of perspectives with the hope of helping America see itself more clearly and heal itself more fully in the wake of the terrorist attack of 9-11-01. From powerful messages to provocative essays to inspirational prayers, these writing reverberate with many of the emotions felt throughout the country.

PREACHING AS CELEBRATION
Homiletics Class on CD and Workbook

Hope for Life International, 2004 / OCLC # 57189238

Since 1989, Thomas has taught doctoral level students, master's level students, preachers in church basements, novice preachers, experienced preachers, seminary, and pastor's conferences. He distills all of this preaching and pastoral experience into *Preaching as Celebration: Homiletics Class on CD and Workbook*, which includes seven sound discs and a small workbook. You may be a novice or an experienced preacher who wants to develop, review, or expand skills in the delivery of God's word. In either case, the materials included herein will be a tremendous blessing in your preaching life.